JUV /REF   Sierra, Judy.
Z
718.3   Twice upon a time.
.S56
1989   **REFERENCE** *cop. 1*

$35.00

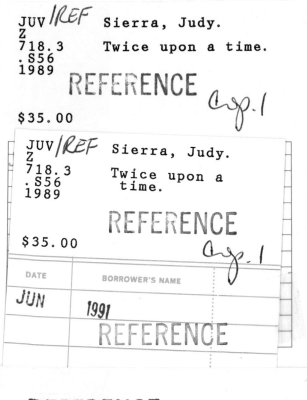

JUV /REF   Sierra, Judy.
Z
718.3   Twice upon a
.S56   time.
1989

REFERENCE

$35.00   *cop. 1*

DATE	BORROWER'S NAME	
JUN	*1991*	
	REFERENCE	

REFERENCE

REFERENCE

REFERENCE

© THE BAKER & TAYLOR CO.

Twice Upon a Time

Twice Upon a Time

by
Judy Sierra and
Robert Kaminski

Stories to Tell ★ Retell ★
Act Out and
Write About

THE H. W. WILSON COMPANY
1989

"Coyote, Iktome, and the Rock" from *American Indian Myths and
Legends*, edited by Richard Erdoes and Alfonso Ortiz. Copyright ©
1984 by Richard Erdoes and Alfonso Ortiz. Reprinted by permission
of Pantheon Books, a Division of Random House, Inc.

"The Liars' Contest" from *The Hat-Shaking Dance and Other Ashanti
Tales from Ghana* by Harold Courlander. Harcourt, Brace and World,
1957. Copyright © by Harold Courlander 1957, 1985.

"Ticky-Picky Boom-Boom" from *Anansi, the Spider Man* by Philip M.
Sherlock. Copyright © 1954 by Philip M. Sherlock. Reprinted by
permission of the author.

Library of Congress Cataloging-in-Publication Data

Sierra, Judy.
    Twice upon a time : stories to tell, retell, act out, and write
about / Judy Sierra, Robert Kaminski.
      p.   cm.
    Bibliography : p.
    ISBN 0-8242-0775-0
    1. Storytelling. 2. Teaching—Aids and devices. 3. Libraries,
Children's—Activity Programs. I. Kaminski, Robert. II. Title.
Z718.3.S56   1989
027.62′51—dc20   89-5696
                                                       CIP

Printed in the United States of America
First Printing

Contents

Preface

There is something about a story. Not just any story . . . but certain ones: folktales, fairy tales, some modern stories and poems. The plots, the characters, the settings come alive for us. We listen, spellbound, to the storyteller. Later, the story replays itself in our head. We may remember it all our lives. Those of us who work with children pass these stories among ourselves, like treasured recipes. Certain stories have the power to unite children and adults in an emotionally satisfying experience. In this sense—and in their ability to calm, excite, and inspire all at the same time—they seem magical.

The authors of this book approach stories both as storytellers and as teachers of the creative arts. We have explored many ways of initiating and motivating children's drama and writing activities. Nothing has ever equaled for us the intensity and excitement generated by a good tale, well told. After hearing a story like "Wiley and the Hairy Man"; or "The Tengu's Magic Nose Fan," children practically leap out of their seats, hands waving, brimming over with ideas for drama, or writing, or illustrating. The emotional and imaginative content of these stories sustains children through long, productive sessions of creative work.

Bruno Bettelheim's claims for the power of traditional tales to speak to the lives of today's children have been borne out time and time again in our work. One need not agree with Bettelheim's Freudian analyses of the tales to acknowledge their power. In these tales a profound artistry and universal sensibility make possible constantly renewed interpretations and meanings.

The inspiration of this book, as well as tens of thousands of hours' experience in classrooms from Anchorage to Zuni, are due in great part to the Artists-in-the-Schools Program of the National Endowment for the Arts. Art thrives where art is funded. Art also thrives in the work of librarian-storytellers like Maggie Darmody, Liz Gooden, Barbara Testa, Judy Kantor, and Jean Pollock, who were all kind enough to share their expertise with us for this book.

Introduction

Students in our college classes and in-service workshops have often expressed dissatisfaction with the books available to them on creative dramatics, creative writing, and storytelling. They would like one practical, "user-friendly" guide that provides both the texts of the best stories for telling and instructions for exciting creative activities based on them.

We have selected from our storytelling repertoire tales that have been consistently successful with child audiences, and which also have the greatest potential to inspire drama and writing activities. These are action stories that can involve the children physically, as well as intellectually and emotionally. All are traditional folktales. Most have undergone changes during the years we have been sharing them; they are our own retellings, shaped by the reactions of many child audiences.

This anthology of stories has been compiled especially for librarians, teachers, drama specialists, recreation leaders, and others who work with children between the ages of eight and twelve. (Tales for children three to eight years old, along with ideas for storytelling and creative dramatics, can be found in Judy Sierra's *The Flannel Board Storytelling Book,* H. W. Wilson, 1987.) When we use the terms "older children" and "younger children," we are referring to children within the eight-to-twelve age range. The twenty stories in the book are arranged in a youngest-to-oldest sequence, but we have not assigned a specific age level to any one story.

Following each story in the book, we include tips for the storyteller and instructions for follow-up creative dramatics and creative writing activities. Activities recommended for a particular story can often be adapted for use with another. When a group has completed several drama or writing projects, the children will begin to offer suggestions for activities; many of the projects in this book began as the children's own ideas.

Three introductory chapters—on storytelling, creative dramatics, and creative writing—explain the techniques we use when we present and lead activities. In a story bibliography, we list fifty more stories and poems for telling and for creative dramatics and creative writing projects.

Our approach to teaching has always been experiential rather than theoretical. We have found that our students learn how to be good storytellers by telling good stories. They learn the techniques of creative dramatics leadership by being led themselves through the steps of a specific activity. They learn to teach creative writing by working with proven and stimulating writing activities. We have attempted to bring the same teaching style to this book, presenting stories and activities chosen and designed to assist group leaders in developing their own talents.

Storytelling

WHY *TELL* STORIES?

Listening to a story told by a storyteller is an intense and exciting experience for a child. For the adult working with children, story*telling* is quite different from story *reading*. The storyteller looks out at the members of the audience, making eye contact, and speaks directly to each of them. Storytelling is an interactive activity in which the children's responses affect the pace, the style, and even the content of the story. For example, a storyteller who sees that children are losing interest in a story is free to make changes in it, based on intuition and knowledge of the group. The storyteller will see and respond to the children's subtle expressions of wonder and excitement, while the story reader will see only the printed page. In children's eyes, the adult who knows stories is a very special person indeed.

All people love to hear stories. Today, television, radio, motion pictures, and books are our society's major storytellers. Yet, a great many of us feel a need and a desire to tell stories as a form of artistic self-expression. The media does not offer opportunities for every would-be storyteller, nor do any of the media provide the rewarding human interaction of live storytelling. Telling to a responsive audience is a joyous experience.

GETTING STARTED

The best first step toward telling stories is to see and hear other storytellers, ideally ones who are telling in a situation that closely resembles your own. This gives you a chance to learn firsthand some of the techniques of storytelling. Storytelling groups exist in many parts of the country. Your local children's librarian may be able to refer you to one, or you can write for a directory to the National Association for the Preservation and Perpetuation of Storytelling, P.O. Box 112, Jonesborough, Tennessee 37659. These groups help you to meet other storytellers in your area and to become aware of special storytelling events in or near your community.

Beginners should start out telling proven stories that are selected from storytelling books and bibliographies or are recommended by experienced tellers. Not all stories that read well tell well. It takes time to develop a sense of what makes a good story for your audience.

LEARNING A STORY

The process of learning a story involves visualization, memorization, and rehearsal. As a rule of thumb, it takes at least two weeks to learn a new story. It is not necessary to spend more than a half hour a day on your story, but the period of two weeks seems to be necessary for the storyteller to become comfortably familiar with the story, to coax it off the printed page and into tellable form.

Most tellers visualize a story; that is, they create

a mental "movie" of it. The storyteller can draw upon these images during the telling of a story, experiencing them as if they were actual memories, and thus helping to make the tale come vividly alive for the audience.

All storytellers use word-for-word memorization, at least for important word patterns, names, and pleasing turns of phrase. Knowing the opening and closing sections of a story *very well* is a necessity. The amount of memorization versus improvisation a storyteller uses in performance depends upon the storyteller and the story. A story written in a unique literary style—one by Rudyard Kipling, for example, or Joseph Jacobs' version of "Jack and the Beanstalk" in this book—requires that the storyteller use as much memorization as possible. Our own technique of learning stories differs. Bob, because of his theater background, memorizes almost all his stories, sparingly making changes based on audience response. Judy approaches the initial learning of the story as if she were memorizing it, then lets it develop and change in rehearsal and performance.

When you use a written source for stories, be aware that there is a difference between effective *literary* language and effective *oral* language. For example, you might be tempted to change the extensive word-for-word repetition used in the story "Buttercup." Such repetition would be inexcusable in a novel for adults or children, yet it delights the listening audience. A reader can scan backwards through a book to refresh his memory; the listener has no such luxury. Repetition is an important technique of storytelling. In the oral tradition, it serves two purposes: it makes learning the story easier for the teller, and it makes following the story easier for the listener. Some other distinctive traits of oral tales are abrupt changes from past tense to present tense during exciting passages, and the use of strings of conjunctions (and . . . but . . . then . . . so . . .) to link sentences.

Once you feel you know a story fairly well, try tape recording yourself as you tell it without the book. Play it back while looking at the text. Mark any important points that you missed, and review them. Make a polished recording of the story, and listen to it as you commute or exercise. Try to tell the story along with the tape. With time, each storyteller devises and perfects the methods of learning and rehearsing a story that work best for him or her.

Tell your first stories as close to the original as possible, observing the effect of the language, the characters, and the plot on the children. The elements of a story that children respond to most enthusiastically may surprise you.

VOICE AND GESTURE IN STORYTELLING

There is no *one* way to tell a story. A storyteller's success is not measured by any critical standards, but by the audience's enjoyment. Dramatic effects that work well on stage before a large audience are usually inappropriate in small, informal settings. For the nonprofessional storyteller, the best technique may be the least technique; in other words, be yourself.

Most classroom audiences will quickly let the teacher know if they cannot hear or understand a story. Storytellers who perform in public, where the audience tends to be more polite, should ask a friend to listen to them from the back of the room. Some common mistakes that interfere with an audience's understanding and appreciation of a story are poor articulation and telling the story too rapidly. If you are dissatisfied with your voice, record your stories on a tape recorder, then critique the telling and record the stories again. There are many good books on voice development, as well as classes and private tutors.

Because your audience is not only listening to you, but also watching you, body language is important in storytelling. Choose a comfortable, relaxed, neutral position from which to tell stories. You needn't remain motionless, of course, but you will put your audience at ease if you always begin and end a gesture, a mime, or other movement, from approximately this position. Some neutral standing positions are hands in pockets of loose-fitting pants or skirt, hands relaxed at your sides, or hands clasped behind your back. Sitting, you can rest your hands in your lap or on your knees. Actions such as gesture and mime, as well as moving around to different parts of the room, can provide enjoyable variety for the storyteller and for the audience. They do need to be thought out in advance and should be used sparingly. Some very good storytellers use hardly any gesture at all.

INTRODUCING THE STORY

For the savvy storytelling audience, "once upon a time," or even simply "once," will signal the beginning of a familiar and pleasurable experience. However, children who are not used to hearing stories will need to be introduced to the basic concept of storytelling. Listeners may miss the entire introduction to a story simply because they are so busy trying to figure out what this strange adult is doing! The section Introducing the Story, which follows each tale in this book, suggests ways to lead children gently into the state of listening to make-believe. An interactive, folklore-based activity such as asking riddles works well. Discussing the "rules" of folktales—how things often happen in threes, for example, or the use of wicked enchantments and spells—will help entice children who might consider themselves too sophisticated to listen to stories.

Certain stories may need more specific introductions. The storyteller might explain the meaning of an unusual word, or briefly introduce a unique character such as Anansi the Spider, or the Russian witch, Baba Yaga. Be aware, however, that not all unusual or new words need to be explained. Many can be adequately understood from context. Ask yourself if understanding a particular word is essential to a listener's understanding or appreciation of the story. Can an explanation wait until after the telling?

Beginning storytellers may be tempted to change unique, antique, and unusual words to common, everyday words. Please don't! Children relish these words and phrases which make the folktale mysterious and special.

PARTICIPATION STORYTELLING

In the section Tips for Storytelling, which also follows each story, we describe some of the specific techniques that have been successful for us when telling that particular tale. Ideas for audience participation, when appropriate, are also included in this section. The storyteller can provide many ways for listeners to join in the storytelling. Younger children will often participate spontaneously, repeating chants and rhymes or mimicking the storyteller's gestures. Most tellers encourage this by smiling and nodding when it happens.

A storyteller who enjoys audience participation can use our suggestions, which follow the stories in this book, or develop her or his own ideas. Participation can be as simple as saying certain words at a cue from the storyteller or singing along during a song. It may be cued by an expectant pause or by a wave of the hand, in the manner of an orchestra conductor. The storyteller will often rehearse participation with the audience before the story begins. Rehearsal should be fun for the audience while serving the storyteller's purpose of making the participation proceed smoothly.

Participation stories are an important part of every storyteller's repertoire. They provide an outlet for restless children who have trouble sitting still and listening. They are particularly useful in working with groups that have limited English proficiency. They are also very popular at parent-child story hours and camp programs, as they work well with groups of widely varying ages.

RETELLING STORIES

Group retelling of a story is an enjoyable follow-up to hearing a story told. In a very informal way, the storyteller begins retelling the story, then asks children to volunteer to tell short segments of the story in sequence, providing transitions as needed. We like using a "magical object," a storytelling stone, for retelling. Ours is a smooth, cool, ocean-polished moonstone that is passed around the circle, transmitting its storytelling powers to each person who holds it. We tell just the very beginning of the story, then hand the stone to the next person in the circle, telling the group that each person can tell just as much or as little of the story as he or she wishes, but that when the stone reaches the very last person, the story will be finished. With practice, a group learns to pace a story among all its members. If someone has taken the story off-track, we take the stone from that child and bring the telling back on course. Any child can choose to simply pass the stone along. When the children know they will be retelling the story—or acting it out, or writing about it—they begin to listen much more carefully.

SOLVING PROBLEMS

Many storytellers feel that they have no time to learn new stories. The problem is more likely that there is too much time. Many of us need a deadline to start our adrenaline flowing and to mobilize our subconscious learning resources. We recommend that during a relatively calm period of the year, you commit yourself publicly to telling a new story on a certain date, at least two weeks in advance. If you are a teacher, announce the event to your class and post it on the bulletin board, or plan with another teacher to exchange storytelling on a certain day. If you are a librarian, plan and publicize a theme story hour featuring the story you are about to learn.

Library storytellers complain of parents bringing noisy toddlers to story hours for older children. The best remedy for this problem is to hold the story hour in a separate room and to enforce an age limit. Library story hours for older children can be successful and well-attended, particularly when they incorporate creative dramatics and creative writing, but usually this is possible *only* if the storyteller can exclude children who are too young.

Librarians also find that many of the older groups that they would like to tell stories to, particularly school groups, are too poorly behaved to listen. If a group won't give the storyteller a chance, the story can't work its magic on them. You may want to consider using a microphone. You can attach a tiny clip-on microphone to your collar, or use a regular microphone on a floor stand, and play your voice through any sound system with an external microphone receptor. Many institutional phonographs and portable radio-cassette players have this feature. The boost in audibility is an effective way of helping your audience hear the story, particularly when there are competing noises (a microphone helps override chatty preschoolers, too). Microphones, microphone stands, and the hardware to adapt them to your sound system are available at low cost from stores that specialize in hobby radio and electronics.

There are always interruptions during storytelling that fall within the range of normal child behavior. Children new to storytelling will often speak out during a story, either with a question or a personal observation. The storyteller has several options, but the purpose of his or her response will be to train the audience to listen quietly. The teller can respond to a comment and then use that response to pull the audience back into the story; ask the child to save the comment until the story is finished; or simply put finger to lips. A group will be more likely to save their comments until the end of a story if the storyteller really does follow through and provide them with an opportunity for discussion and questions.

Once when Judy was telling the story "Baba Yaga" at a library, a boy of about ten arrived late and was just sitting down at the point in the story where Baba Yaga's cat begins weaving. His loud and very annoyed voice broke the silence. "Do you expect me to believe *that*?" "No," was Judy's immediate thought, "I sincerely hope that you don't." But instead, she said, "This is a fairy tale. Do you like to hear fairy tales?" The boy nodded and settled back down. He had missed the introduction to the story, in which the children are told that they are about to hear a fairy tale; he obviously needed this reassurance.

Interruptions are dealt with kindly but firmly. A storyteller who finds frequent interruptions disturbing should consider shorter stories, ones with more participation, or ones with more exciting plots and language.

A storyteller may find an audience disappointingly unresponsive. It could be that the teller's style or the stories' content is perceived by the group as too juvenile. A well-chosen story that is suited to a group's age level should draw in the most resistant non-listener. The beginning storyteller should be aware, too, that a glassy-eyed, faraway expression can be a sign of a child's utter absorption in a story.

A LAST WORD TO STORY READERS

Should you remain, despite our urgings, a non-storyteller, please read the stories in this book aloud. Read them with verve and enthusiasm! From time to time, mark your place with your finger, look out at your audience, and tell a part of the story in your own words.

BIBLIOGRAPHY

Bauer, Caroline Feller. *A Handbook for Storytellers.* Chicago: American Library Association, 1977.

> An encyclopedic resource guide to sharing books and stories with children, *A Handbook for Storytellers* is particularly valuable for its descriptions of ways in which props, puppets, magic tricks, etc., may be used to enhance storytelling.

MacDonald, Margaret Read. *The Storyteller's Sourcebook: A Subject, Title and Motif Index to Folklore Collections for Children.* Chicago: Gale/Neal Schuman, 1982.

> This is an indispensable reference tool for locating children's versions of folktales in collections. MacDonald has adapted Stith Thompson's system of classifying the motifs of folktales, enabling the storyteller to find not only a particular story, but also similar stories from other countries and cultures.

MacDonald, Margaret Read. *Twenty Tellable Tales: Audience Participation Folktales for the Beginning Storyteller.* New York: H. W. Wilson, 1986.

> The twenty tales in this book are generally for younger children. MacDonald places the words of the stories on the

page in a way that aids the beginning storyteller in learning and interpreting the story.

Schimmel, Nancy. *Just Enough to Make a Story.* Berkeley, Calif.: Sisters' Choice Press, 1982.

This slim paperback packs more wisdom and advice for storytellers into fifty-plus pages than others do in hundreds. Schimmel draws on experience as a children's librarian and professional entertainer, and she offers ideas for telling and selecting stories to suit a wide range of personal storytelling styles.

Stories: A List of Stories to Tell and to Read Aloud. Compiled by Marilyn Berg Iarusso. New York: New York Public Library, 1977.

This annotated bibliography of good tales for telling includes storytelling recordings and an index of stories by country.

Creative Dramatics

The fourth-graders are crouched low, hiding behind their desks. All are playing the role of Buttercup, a plump little Norwegian child who is the intended dinner of the local troll. Two girls have chosen to play Buttercup's mother. They stand at a table, stirring up an imaginary cake. The teacher knocks three times on her desk.

"Good morning," croons the teacher/troll in mock sweetness. "Is your little Buttercup at home today?"

"Nooooo." The mothers shake their heads. "He's out hunting with his father."

"The plague take it!" cries the troll. Then, regaining her composure, "I have the nicest little silver knife for him."

"Pip! Pip! Here I am!" Up pop the children playing Buttercup.

"Oh, Buttercup, I have the nicest little silver knife for you here in my sack. But I am so old, and my back is so stiff, you will have to climb inside and get it yourself."

Shifting to narration, the teacher guides the children as they mime climbing into the troll's sack, imagining what it is like to be inside the sack while the troll runs along the forest path. They wait as the troll lays the sack down, and then listen for the sound of the troll's snoring before cutting a hole in the bag with a little silver knife.

After listening to their teacher tell the story of "Buttercup," the group had discussed the story and reviewed the dialogue of the opening scene. The teacher decided to use the technique of multiple casting so that all the children could be involved at once. This introductory creative dramatics session lasted about twenty minutes, including planning time. The next day, the children asked to play the same scene again. Afterward, they chose another part of the story to act out.

WHAT IS CREATIVE DRAMATICS?

Creative dramatics uses no script and is not destined for an audience. It resembles children's free play and games, pantomime and improvisation. Like a game, it has rules that keep it going smoothly. It has an adult leader who plans, coaches, and facilitates the playing sessions. In the creative dramatics projects in this book, we use children's love of play and pretending to involve them in thinking about and experiencing literature.

Extending stories into play is a natural progression. Many families do this spontaneously, playing "The Three Billy Goats Gruff" on a footbridge, for example, or acting out "The Three Bears" at the breakfast table. Such kinesthetic and imaginative involvement with story may be an important prerequisite for becoming a reader of literature. Beyond merely comprehending individual words, a reader creates feelings and images from the words he or she reads. One very effective way an adult can teach this skill to children is through drama.

Creative dramatics extends literature into play and brings playfulness to literature. We have found that folktales, with their strong, clear plots, characters, and emotions, provide excellent material for creative dramatics.

Another important benefit of creative dramatics is social and behavioral. The spirit of group cooperation and responsibility that can be achieved in an ongoing creative dramatics program is remarkable. Teachers especially comment that creative dramatics gives every child a feeling of accomplishment and satisfaction, as well as a chance for peer recognition of their talents.

For group leaders who plan eventually to have children put on plays for an audience, creative dramatics offers the ideal pretheater training; it teaches concentration, body awareness, and teamwork.

PLANNING FOR CREATIVE DRAMATICS ACTIVITIES

The materials required for creative dramatics are few. Props and costumes are not necessary; in fact, they are not recommended. All that is needed is an open playing area in which children can sit in a circle and move around freely. In a room that lacks an open space, such as a classroom or library, plan and rehearse moving the furniture aside quickly and quietly. Doing this well is a creative dramatics exercise in itself. With concentration, teamwork, and self-control, a group of children can clear a creative dramatics space with hardly any noise at all. A stage or auditorium can be used, but be sure to form a creative dramatics circle, not the theater arrangement of performers on one side and observers on the other. Younger children can work outdoors, though older children may be uncomfortable if they are in a place where others can see them.

Ideally, beginning creative dramatics sessions should be frequent and short, even as brief as five minutes. If the leader is committed to a longer time period, the program can be extended with participation storytelling and games during the first few introductory sessions. For an experienced group, an hour of creative dramatics seems to fly by.

The ideal number of children for creative dramatics is twelve to fifteen, of nearly the same age. In our experience, it usually takes a minimum of twelve children to generate a group dynamic that minimizes self-consciousness. Larger numbers are manageable if the children know each other and are used to working together.

THE CREATIVE DRAMATICS LEADER

A playful spirit, a lively imagination, and dedication to children's creative expression are probably the most important qualifications of the creative dramatics leader. By planning a continuing series of short sessions, the leader gains time to develop the skills necessary to work in this medium. The goal is always to keep the children "on task"; this means choosing appropriate activities, introducing and leading them in a way that motivates the children, and being flexible enough to change gears if things are not going as expected.

Select activities that you think your group will

enjoy, then visualize the activities. Prepare notecards to use during the creative dramatics session to remind yourself of the activities you have chosen and of their sequence. Be sure to plan more activities than will probably be needed.

BASIC RULES FOR CREATIVE DRAMATICS

The leader should introduce the children to these rules before beginning the first creative dramatics session.

Freeze rule. The leader has the prerogative to call "freeze" at any time. The signal for freeze can be calling out the word "freeze," or using a metal clicker or other small noisemaker. The clicker, a little metal gadget usually in the shape of an animal, will fit in a pocket and can be used with one hand to make a loud, attention-getting noise.

The leader usually calls freeze when the drama activities have gotten out of control (are too noisy, for example), or when it is time for a transition to a new activity.

At the beginning of your first creative dramatics session, have the children practice freezing until they can do it quickly and well. Begin by telling them to move around the room and talk—perhaps counting or reciting the alphabet—then give the freeze signal. Repeat this until they can do it to your satisfaction three times in a row.

No directing rule. The leader or the group may decide *who* plays which role in a drama activity, *what* things will happen, and *where,* but no one may dictate anyone else *how* to do anything. That is decided by each individual, pair, or small group. Deciding the *how* for oneself is the creative part of the creative dramatics.

Closure rule. All sessions will end with closure, in which the leader summarizes what was done and the children can evaluate the activities and suggest ideas for future sessions.

No blame rule. In any discussion of the creative dramatics activities, neither the leader nor the participants may blame anyone else in the group. The leader should also refrain from praising individuals, especially *during* the drama session. Praise for the group can be expressed during closure.

MUSICAL INSTRUMENTS

Though creative dramatics uses no props or costumes, a collection of inexpensive musical instruments can add greatly to the success of drama activities. We recommend using a drum in many of the warm-ups and beginning drama activities. Rhythm makes moving and miming in character much easier for children. Also, the leader can control and vary the pace of the activity with a drum. We suggest you obtain a handheld drum, one that looks like a tambourine without the jangles; these are available at music stores. Other instruments that come in handy are wood blocks (or claves), kazoo, triangle, small xylophone, maracas, and any other children's or ethnic musical instruments you can find. Children use these instruments to provide sound effects in the participation activity suggested for the story "How Fire Came to Earth" in this collection. Other activities can be enhanced by sound effects provided either by the leader or by children in the group.

WARM-UPS

Warm-ups are gamelike exercises used to begin creative dramatics sessions. Their purpose is to provide a transition from the world of the everyday into the world of imagination. They help to overcome self-consciousness and encourage teamwork. All creative dramatics sessions, even for advanced groups, should begin with one or more warm-up activities. The following are beginning warm-ups, which may be used to introduce groups to creative dramatics.

Tossing Imaginary Objects

As the group sits or stands in a circle, the leader shows the group an imaginary softball, then makes eye contact with a child at the other side of the circle. When the leader is sure that the intended catcher knows who he or she is, the leader tosses the ball across to that child, who then makes eye contact with someone else and throws the ball to him, and so on.

Let this continue until some of the children begin to show some different styles of throwing. Then, have the child with the ball throw it to you. Tell the group that this is a magic ball. It can be made larger or smaller, heavier or lighter. Each child who catches the ball reshapes it—into a Ping-Pong ball, or a beach ball, or a bowling ball, for example—before tossing it. Each is to handle and throw the ball in a way that shows how large and how heavy it is. The child who catches the ball also shows its present size and weight before changing it. Younger children may need help from the leader, in the form of guiding narration, in order to create and maintain illusions. The leader might say, "Now he's making the ball bigger. Is it heavy or light? [pause for the child to show—not tell] Oh, it's heavy. It's so heavy he can hardly lift it. How will he ever be able to throw it?" The leader uses narration carefully to lead the children into their own discoveries, not to tell them what to do.

Mirror Exercise

The mirror exercise is extremely effective for overcoming self-consciousness. Pair off (leader can be part of a pair) and face each other. One member of each pair is designated as the "real person," the other as the mirror image. One child mirrors the other as closely as possible. Coach the children to move very slowly. The goal is not to fool the other person, but to have two people moving in precise synchronization. Have the members of the pairs switch roles.

As a variation on the mirror exercise, each pair decides secretly which one of them is the mirror image, and they try to fool the leader.

Jumping Jack Freeze

Everyone in the group starts doing jumping jacks. The leader calls out the name of an animal, a story character, an athletic activity, etc., then beats on the drum three times. On the third beat, everyone must freeze in the shape of whatever the leader called out. Children like to see how long they can remain perfectly still, but don't stretch this to the point where they begin to collapse! The leader can circulate and comment on the "garden of statues."

Machine

The machine activity is the ultimate in cooperation. Begin by asking the children to name types of machines, then to name various moving parts a machine might have. Ask for volunteers to demonstrate how a machine part might move, then ask the whole group to perform the action. Add noises that the part might make.

Tell the children they are going to go to the center of the circle, one at a time, and build a machine. Each child will be a part of the machine. Each part will move, and it will also make a noise. The parts will not touch, but they will seem to move together. Use a drumbeat to set the rhythm of the machine, and send the children one at a time to join in.

With your drum, pounding softly so as not to drown out the machine noises, change the tempo of the machine. Explain that there is an energy shortage, or that a cloud has covered the solar panels that power the machine, as you slow it down very gradually to a stop. You can end the activity in a quiet manner at this point, or go further, with maintenance workers coming in to repair the machine. With your narration, instruct a repair crew to tighten bolts, oil parts, check the wiring, refill the gas tank, or whatever is needed to keep the machine in good working order. After the repair crew has completed its work, send in a crew of inspectors with imaginary clipboards and checklists to make sure all the work has been done correctly. Then gradually bring the machine back up to speed.

For an energetic ending, speed up the tempo of the machine with your drumbeat, and, playing the role of the factory foreman, talk about the need for greater and greater productivity. One by one, lightly tap the machine "parts" as you describe how they explode, fly off the machine, and return to their original position on the parts shelf (that is, in the creative dramatics circle).

Children love making machines again and again. You can add variety and motivation by making the machine a housecleaning machine, a money-making machine, a homework machine, etc.

BEGINNING CREATIVE DRAMATICS ACTIVITIES

The creative dramatics activities described after each story in this book are given in easiest-to-hardest order. In the simplest exercises, the children work individually or in pairs, usually pantomiming actions to the leader's narration. In this narration the leader is careful to motivate the children without telling them *how* to move or act. The leader and the children are a team—together they recreate the tale. The leader describes part of what is happening, and the children show the rest. There need never be a situation in which the children are merely following directions.

Movement such as walking increases concentration. The leader can help children to develop their characters while they are still seated, encouraging them to become aware—if they are giants, for example—of their huge feet, legs, arms, hands, and heads. Sometimes we have the children close their eyes, and we describe them slowly waking up as a character in the story. By the time they are standing, they have begun to imagine their body differently. Younger children can walk in a circle, to the beat of the drum, as the leader narrates:

> The giant is very hungry. He is starving. He is sniffing and smelling, looking around every-where for something to eat. You see something delicious. Pick it up and eat it like a giant.

At this point, the leader can interview the children, asking each what he or she found to eat.

Older children can walk in a random fashion around the room, developing their feeling for a character as they experiment with different kinds of movement. Each responds individually to narration by the leader. Specific ways of leading movement exercises in character are described after each story.

Individual mimes and pair mimes involve responding to the leader's narration of a part of the story. Each child or pair of children is playing the same character or pair of characters at the same time. Jack waking up, seeing the beanstalk, deciding to grab onto it, then climbing up to the sky, would be an example of a leader-narrated individual mime. An example of a pair mime would be Jack showing his mother the magic beans, and his mother reacting. During these activities everyone in the group is acting; no one is watching. The leader improvises and paces the narration based on an assessment of the children's involvement.

SCENE PLAY

The best scenes for dramatization are those that include either a task to be accomplished or a conflict to be resolved. For the children involved in these scenes, there is the motivation of a problem to be solved in the process of playing. These may be actual scenes from the story, or madeup scenes that explore events before or after the story. Scene play will always be preceded by planning and discussion. The relevant parts of the story can be retold in order to refresh the players' memories. Decisions will need to be made about the use of the playing space to represent places in the scene.

When acting out scenes with a large group, say a class of twenty-five or more children, the leader can use the techniques of multiple casting; that is, having more than one person playing the same role at the same time, as we described in the dramatization of "Buttercup." Multiple casting works best with younger groups. The leader may choose to play a role in the scene in order to help motivate the children. We have found that children readily accept a leader's switching back and forth between a role in the scene and a role as narrator.

A large group can watch as smaller groups play a series of scenes in the center of the playing space. The cast should be changed at the beginning of each scene. For example, in playing "Jack and the Beanstalk," there could be a different child playing the parts of Jack, the ogre, and the ogre's wife each time Jack goes to the top of the beanstalk. It is often enjoyable, even necessary, to have children play the part of animals or inanimate objects, such as the ogre's singing harp.

Older and experienced players can work on scenes independently in small groups and then share their work with the whole group after they have refined it. As children advance to this stage, be sure that they follow the "no directing" rule, so that one child does not take control of the group. When children begin working independently, they often ask to use props and costumes. We have found that the use of props and costumes leads to long delays as they are prepared, repaired, misplaced, etc. We try to encourage children to put on plays at home, stressing that creative dramatics is a different type of activity with different ground rules.

SOLVING PROBLEMS

If your group seems apathetic, they could be afraid to risk entering into the drama process. Try involving them in more warm-ups and dramatic games. See the bibliography for additional resources.

A group that is enthusiastic about creative dramatics, but is stuck at the level of parody and showing off, may be working with stories that are too young for them. Challenge their talents with activities such as the character mimes in "The Liar's Contest" or the sleeping and waking sequence in "Briar Rose." Or, express your dissatisfaction at a group closure session and ask the group for help in solving the problem.

If you have trouble maintaining control of the creative dramatic sessions, keep your sessions extremely short. "Leave them wanting more" is an old show business expression. A group of children with behavior problems can benefit from several months of concentration solely on warm-up activities.

BIBLIOGRAPHY

Harbin, E. O. *Games of Many Nations*. New York: Abingdon Press, 1954.

> Many traditional children's games are mini-dramas. The games in this collection are listed by country, and some are suitable for as many as thirty players. They would make a perfect addition to a creative dramatics session. See also Nina Millen's *Children's Games from Many Lands* (New York: Friendship Press, 1965).

Heinig, Ruth Beall, and Lyda Stillwell. *Creative Dramatics for the Classroom Teacher*. Englewood Cliffs, N.J.: Prentice-Hall, 1974.

> This is the best comprehensive book on creative dramatics for the elementary teacher. Instructions are clearly presented, and the activities are related to classroom and curriculum goals.

Novelly, Maria C. *Theatre Games for Young Performers*. Colorado Springs, Co.: Meriwether, 1985.

> Though intended for young adults, ages twelve to fifteen, most of these theater games can be used as they are or be slightly adapted for younger groups. The games are contemporary and clearly presented.

Spolin, Viola. *Improvisation for the Theater*. Evanston, Ill.: Northwestern University Press, 1963.

Viola Spolin is the originator of "theater games." Her aim is to prepare actors for the theater, so you will need to ignore her references to "sharing with the audience." There are wonderful exercises here for children, although the section describing her work with children is disappointing and can be skipped. Use this book as a resource for warm-up activities.

Creative Writing

The purpose of the creative writing activities in this book is to stimulate writing for personal enjoyment and for fluency. It is very easy for a child to move from listening to a story into a writing activity based on that story, since the stimulus for writing has been recent, and it has been verbal. These writing exercises are not meant to be graded, though they can be read aloud, displayed on a bulletin board, or shared and appreciated in other ways. We have found that many children are willing to read their work to the group, and that most are extremely eager to have us read their work aloud—usually anonymously. Many of the writing projects we describe include art; some are individual exercises and some are group activities. All inspire a high level of enjoyment and enthusiasm which make them perfect for library and recreation programs as well as classrooms.

ROLE OF THE LEADER

The role of the leader in creative writing activities varies with the age of the children. Young and beginning writers need the experience of first creating a piece of writing as a group. In the process of group writing, the leader uses a chalkboard (or a large tablet of paper on an easel) to write down the children's ideas.

Group writing begins with brainstorming. After the leader has explained the project to the group, ideas contributed by the children are written on the board, without evaluation or judgment. When all ideas have been expressed (or when they are beginning to get repetitive, or when the leader decides to call time), the writing begins. The leader selects bits and pieces of the children's ideas to fit into the form of the project, writing the final product on the board. The leader "thinks aloud," telling the children why certain words and phrases are selected and also taking suggestions from the group. Each child then copies the group writing from the board. The leader may choose to encourage them to make changes and additions of their own as they copy.

A step beyond group writing is individual writing preceded by group brainstorming. The teacher writes children's ideas on the board as above. Then each student creates his or her own composition, using the words and ideas that have been written on the board in any way he or she chooses.

The leader can choose to have children work on some writing projects together in pairs or in small groups, with one of them acting as secretary.

TYPES OF WRITING ACTIVITIES

Non-Narrative Writing

These short writing projects are especially useful for library groups, recreation groups, mixed-age groups, and younger children. Many include art; for example, creating a comic strip of a part of a story, making a story map, writing a short poem or magic spell, drawing a wanted poster or advertisement. In some instances, the leader will want to provide samples to help the children conceptualize the activity. For example, we suggest that the group make seed packets, complete with planting and growing instructions, for the magic beans from "Jack and the Beanstalk." Many children have never seen a seed package, and the leader will need to provide some for the children to examine before beginning their projects. When children create comic strip art, it is helpful to provide them with paper that has squares already drawn onto it. Paper of unusual size and color can help inspire art and writing projects.

Beginning Narrative Writing

Short narrative projects for beginning writers include

writing a letter as one of the characters in a story, or telling some part of the events of the story in the first person; writing a diary entry as one of the characters; telling a part of the story in a different format, such as newspaper article, television news report, or script; telling something else that happened to a story character before or after the actual events in the story.

These are only very general categories; we always present a specific "story-starter" to the group to engage their imaginations. When this is done in a vivid and artistic way, it is called guided imagery. See "Flea's-eye View" with the story "The Nungwama" for an example of this technique. We often suggest, and write on the board, the first few words or the first sentence of the writing activity. Children are free to use them or not, as they wish.

Advanced Narrative Writing

Advanced creative writing projects include re-writing a story from one character's point of view and writing a parallel story.

When asking children to write from the point of view of one of the characters, we have found it wise to leave the choice up to them. While *we* might find a villain's-eye-view most intriguing, many children are incapable of identifying with a character they don't like. It is interesting to experiment with using the point of view of a character who is not in the original story, such as a flea on the top of a monster's head in "Flea's-eye View," following "The Nungwama."

In writing a parallel story, the children are asked to imagine the story with one element changed. Usually, this means that another protagonist has similar adventures, as in the writing exercise we describe following "Wiley and the Hairy Man." In this tale, the Hairy Man must be tricked three times before he will leave you alone. We describe a situation in which another young person, a girl this time, encounters the Hairy Man. Children who have been given this exercise have been quite resourceful in devising new ways to trick the Hairy Man and in writing a structurally complete story.

After children have been exposed to a series of stories and writing projects, give them an opportunity to do free writing in a session where the only directive is to write a story.

We have found that activities based on folktales could not be better training for young writers. Folktales have a strong and predictable structure, and learning structure is an important part of learning to write. Because structure is so tight in folktales, we discourage the assignment of writing a new ending to a tale. In a highly polished folktale, or well-crafted literary tale, the ending is inevitable. The listener is prepared for the ending from the very beginning, so changing it would be illogical.

SOLVING PROBLEMS

We have had surprisingly few problems with children not wanting to write, or feeling inadequate as writers. Using folktales as a stimulus seems to generate a high level of enthusiasm. If the leader accepts all efforts, and provides a resource pool of words and phrases on the board through the technique of brainstorming, there should be adequate encouragement and raw material for everyone. Often, children are so excited about what they are writing that they switch from English to their native language halfway through an activity. Others bring us the writing they are doing at home.

Children sometimes want to use their writing

activities to make fun of other people in the class, or to show how many musical groups they can name, and so on—especially if the leader will be reading the papers aloud. They may just need to get a certain amount of parodying and playing out of their system before they can approach writing with greater concentration. If we are going to be reading papers to the class, we screen them first. If we find names of other children or unacceptable language, we return them to the authors in a nonjudgmental way for revision. When deciding what content is acceptable, the leader needs to keep in mind that the children may be making insightful parallels between the content of the story and their own world. Therefore, it's best to consider carefully before outlawing references to television, movies, or current events.

BIBLIOGRAPHY

Clark, Roy Peter. *Free to Write: A Journalist Teaches Young Writers*. London: Heinemann, 1987.

> This is an excellent, comprehensive guide to teaching the process of writing to children. It is equally useful to the beginning teacher of writing and to the seasoned instructor.

Moffett, James. *Active Voice: A Writing Program Across the Curriculum*. Montclair, N.J.: Boynton/Cook, 1981.

> This practical companion to the author's *Coming on Center* (below) is brimming with ideas for writing for children nine and older. These assignments are sequenced to correspond to children's intellectual and emotional growth. Moffett explains how the young writer can take his or her chaotic inner voice and transform it into a finished product suitable for an audience.

————. *Coming on Center: English Education in Evolution.* Montclair, N.J.: Boynton/Cook, 1981.

Coming on Center argues for language arts and literacy programs, in communities as well as in schools, that place equal emphasis on reading, writing, listening, speaking, and performing. Moffett provides an approach to improving skills that does not rely on drills and rules. In a concise and readable style, he demonstrates how the use of storytelling, poetry, movement, and improvisation will improve literacy.

Rico, Gabriele Lusser. *Writing the Natural Way: Using Right-Brain Techniques to Release Your Expressive Powers.* Los Angeles: J. P. Tarcher, 1983.

Rico's book is a resource for the brainstorming technique known as "clustering," which has been used successfully with child writers. Chapter two is especially useful.

Ticky-Picky Boom-Boom

JAMAICA

At last the famine was over. The rains came. First heavy black clouds covered the sky, and then the rain came down in floods. The dry earth seemed to drink up the rain until it could drink no more. The parched brown grass became green. Life started again, and everyone began to plant.

Even Anansi set to work. Never before had he worked so hard or so long. At last the large square of land around his house was full of yams and potatoes. Now the yams were ready. Anansi looked out from his window at the field of yams and said to himself, "I must have a garden with flowers in it, like a rich man. I will get Tiger to come and dig up the yams for me."

Anansi went to Tiger and said, "Good morning, Mr. Tiger. I hope you are very well. I beg you to come with your hoe and machete and dig my yams."

"What will you give me?" asked Tiger, stroking his mustache and looking hard at Anansi. He was beginning to be a little suspicious of this Anansi, who always got the better of him.

"I will give you all the yams that you dig up," said Anansi.

That was fair enough, thought greedy Mr. Tiger. Next morning he went to Anansi's house early with his hoe and machete; and he dug and dug; and the more he dug, the more the yams seemed to grow down into the ground. By and by four o'clock came, working time was over, and Tiger had not dug up a single yam.

Tiger was angry. He looked at the yams and the deep holes that he had dug around them, and he thought of how hard and long he had worked, and he could keep his temper no longer. Tiger took his machete and chopped at one of the yams with it. He chopped into little pieces as much of the yam as he could reach, and then he set off for home.

What was that? There was a noise behind him. Tiger looked around, and he saw all the yams coming after him.

Some of the yams had one leg, some had two legs, some had three legs, some had four legs.

And the noise their feet made as they came stamping and running down the road sounded like this:

Ticky-Picky Boom-Boom,
Ticky-Picky Boom-Boom, Boof!

Tiger began to run. The yams ran, too. Tiger began to gallop. The yams galloped, too. Tiger jumped. The yams jumped. Tiger made for Brother Dog's house as fast as he could, and he called out at the top of his voice, "Oh, Brother Dog, Brother Dog, hide me from the yams."

Dog said, "All right, Tiger, hide behind me and don't say a word."

So Tiger hid behind Dog.

Down the road came the yams, stamping on their two legs, three legs, four legs:

Ticky-Picky Boom-Boom,
Ticky-Picky Boom-Boom, Boof!

And they said, "Brother Dog, did Tiger go this way?"

Mr. Dog looked straight ahead and said, "You know, Mr. Yam, I can't see Mr. Tiger at all."

But Tiger could not keep still. He was so frightened that he called out, "Don't tell them, Mr. Dog!" And Mr. Dog was so angry that he ran away and left Tiger.

And the yams jumped.

And Tiger jumped.

And the yams ran, and Tiger ran.

The yams galloped, and Tiger galloped.

Then Tiger saw Sister Duck and all the little ducklings by the side of the pond. Tiger hurried to her as fast as he could and cried, "Sister Duck, hide me, hide me from the yams that are coming."

"All right, Tiger," she said. "Get behind me, but don't say a word."

So Tiger hid behind Sister Duck.

By and by the yams came stamping along.

Ticky-Picky Boom-Boom,
Ticky-Picky Boom-Boom, Boof!

And the yams said, "Sister Duck, have you seen Tiger?"

Sister Duck looked straight ahead and said, "I can't see him, Yams, I can't see him at all."

But Tiger was so frightened that he called out, "Don't tell them, Sister Duck, don't tell them!"

And Sister Duck was so angry that she moved away and left him to the yams.

And the yams jumped, and Tiger jumped.

And the yams ran, and Tiger ran.

And the yams galloped, and Tiger galloped.

Tiger was growing tired. Always he could hear the yams coming behind him. At last he came to a little stream, and over it there was a plank of wood. On the other side was Mr. Goat.

Tiger ran across the plank as fast as he could and he cried, "Oh, my Brother Goat, hide me from the yams that are coming."

"All right, Tiger, but you must not say a word."

So Tiger hid behind Goat.

The yams came stamping down the road:

Ticky-Picky Boom-Boom,
Ticky-Picky Boom-Boom, Boof!

When they reached the little bridge they called out, "Mr. Goat, have you seen Tiger?"

Mr. Goat looked straight ahead, but before he could say a word Tiger called out, "Don't tell them, Mr. Goat, don't tell them."

The yams jumped onto the wooden plank and tried to cross; but Goat put his head down and butted them, one after another, so that they all fell into the river and were broken to pieces.

Brother Tiger and Brother Goat picked up all the pieces and went off to Tiger's home to have a great feast.

And they never asked Anansi to the feast of yams.

And sometimes, when the night is dark, Tiger still feels frightened when he hears someone stamping down the forest track with a noise that sounds like:

Ticky-Picky Boom-Boom,
Ticky-Picky Boom-Boom, Boof!

INTRODUCING THE STORY

Anansi the spider is a tricky fellow. Many stories are told about him in West Africa and among people of African heritage in the New World. Some children may already have heard stories about Anansi. Two other Anansi stories are included in this book: "How Anansi Got a Small Waist" and "The Liars' Contest."

However, Anansi is not the most important character in this story. A foolish tiger shares the spotlight with a group of very mean yams. If the children are not familiar with yams, the storyteller will probably want to show some to the group. After the storytelling, the yams can become part of a cooking project, and the group can pretend to join Tiger and Mr. Goat in their feast of yams.

"Ticky-Picky Boom-Boom" begins with a great rainstorm, so we like to begin the storytelling session with group-participation rainmaking. Ask the children to join in and imitate your actions, so that you can all make a rainstorm together.

Have you ever been on top of a high hill or a mountain, and seen dark rainclouds in the distance? Let's imagine we are sitting on top of a grassy hill. Feel the soft grass. Feel the cool breeze blowing on your face. Off in the distance, you see tall, dark clouds—thunderheads. The wind is blowing the clouds closer and closer. You begin to hear the sound of the rain. [Rub your palms together, gently, around and around. This doesn't make much of a sound until a group of people do it together.] Now the rain is beginning to fall all around you. [Tap two fingers of each hand together to make the sound of the raindrops.] The rain is falling harder now. [Tap four fingers together.] Now the rain is pouring down! [Clap your hands together.] Listen to the thunder. [Clap harder, then stop and wait for the group to quiet down.] Now the storm is moving away, and the rain is falling more softly. [Tap four fingers of each hand together, now two, now rub your palms together, place your hands in your lap and begin the story.]

TIPS FOR STORYTELLING

The repetitive nature of the chant, the dialogue, and the episodes make "Ticky-Picky Boom-Boom" an easy story to learn. A strong visualization of the locale—a sort of aerial map—will assist the storyteller's memory. This tale also provides an opportunity for the storyteller to use the character voices children love so well. Sister Duck, Brother

Dog, and Mr. Goat can each have a distinctive voice based on the corresponding animal noise. A trick of professional voice-over actors is to use a "hook," a special word or sound, as the basis for each voice. For example, Brother Dog can begin each sentence with a short "rrrufff," which sets his voice quality. The storyteller keeps his or her mouth in that "rrrufff" shape and barks out Brother Dog's words. Sister Duck would use a "quack," and Mr. Goat a bleating noise. It is important to use character voices selectively in story-telling. They tend to focus the attention of the audience on the storyteller's skill rather than on the story. The storyteller who is not an actor or actress can effectively use his or her own voice for all major characters, changing voice for comic or scary ones.

Participation Storytelling

The audience enjoys chanting "ticky-picky boom-boom" along with the storyteller, perhaps also clapping their hands rhythmically on their knees as they say it. We tell the children the name of the story, then ask them to repeat it with us several times. Then, when the chant comes up in the story, we pause, smile and begin saying it slowly, using eye contact to let them know we want them to join in.

CREATIVE DRAMATICS

Warm-ups

Walking as the characters in the story can be done by the group either as a warm-up for further creative dramatic activity or as an activity in itself.

Begin with a discussion of the characters. What does each one look like? How do they act in the story? Ask for volunteers to show the way each character might walk. Then, have the group stand and walk in a circle to the soft beat of the leader's drum, and narrate their walk.

> Walk like Mr. Tiger. You feel good. Anansi is giving you all his yams. Swing your tail. [Allow time for the group to become absorbed in the activity before making a transition.] Now, walk like Sister Duck, waddling down the path. All your ducklings are behind you. You have to protect them. Be on the lookout for danger. Now, you are walking through the mud, now walk down into the pond and start to swim. . . .

Action Mimes

Many of the characters' actions adapt well to individual mimes. As the leader narrates, the children all play the part of Anansi planting his garden, then Tiger trying to dig up the yams, then Mr. Goat butting the yams into the air, and then Tiger trying to fall asleep at night while imagining that the yams are still chasing him.

Scene Play

Always begin scene play with retelling the story. Children enjoy acting out the scenes in which Tiger asks for help from Sister Duck, then Brother Dog, then Mr. Goat.

Designate parts of the playing space to represent Anansi's garden, Duck's pond, Dog's house, and Mr. Goat's stream. Select children to play the parts of Anansi, Tiger, Sister Duck and her ducklings, Brother Dog, and Mr. Goat. The remaining children may play the yams. Everyone takes his place: the yams crouch low, pretending to be in the ground, and Mr. Tiger begins to chop the air above their heads. Scene play begins. During the chase scenes, the yams and Tiger run in place.

CREATIVE WRITING

Drawing a Story Map

Begin by working as a group to remember all the places named in the story, and list them on the chalkboard. The children may wish to give special names to these places, such as "Yam Creek." The children then draw maps of Tiger's neighborhood, including and labeling all the important places he went to on the day of the story: Tiger's house, Anansi's house, Anansi's garden, Brother Dog's place, Sister Duck's pond, Brother Goat's house, the stream, and the wooden plank across it. They will need to show the road Tiger and the yams ran along that connects all these places. The story map may also be a large group project, with different children or groups of children working on the various parts of the map.

How I Harvested Anansi's Yams

Imagine that Anansi has asked *you* to dig up his yams. As you dig, the yams tunnel deeper and deeper into the earth. But, unlike Tiger, you outsmarted the yams and took them home in a sack. Begin your story with the sentence, 'The more I dug for those yams, the deeper and deeper they seemed to tunnel into the ground. Then I had an idea.'

Evening News Script

You are a reporter on the evening news. You want to tell the TV audience about the extraordinary things that happened to Tiger today. Write the story in six to ten very exciting sentences. You don't have to tell the whole story. Be sure to quote Tiger saying how he felt when the yams were chasing him.

This writing activity should be shared orally by any children who want to read their scripts like a real news reporter. Supporting props, such as a microphone, a mock TV camera, or actual videotaping, help focus the children's attention and add to their enjoyment.

The Tengu's Magic Nose Fan

JAPAN

Badger was walking through the forest one morning. He had spent the previous night gambling with some of his friends, and he had won a lot of money. The pack on his back was filled with coins, and with good things to eat. In his hand, he held a sweet rice cake. As he walked deeper into the forest, Badger heard a noise:

"Hee, hee, hee, hee, hee!"

Badger followed the noise to a small clearing among the pine trees. There, he saw some tengu children playing with a fan. One of the children would fan his nose, and the nose would grow, and grow, and grow, and grow, until—*bump!*—it hit a tree. Then the little tengu would flip the fan over and fan and fan his nose with the other side, and his nose would shrink, and shrink, and shrink, and shrink, and shrink, until it was a small, regular-sized nose again. Then all the little tengus would laugh:

"Hee, hee, hee, hee, hee!"

Badger watched the tengu children play with their fan, and he thought to himself, "If *I* had that fan, I could make myself a lot of money."

Badger stepped forward into the clearing.

"Children! Little tengu children! I have a sweet

rice cake for each one of you. Just close your eyes and hold out your hand.''

The tengu children rushed forward. They closed their eyes, and each held out a hand.

"I have *two* sweet rice cakes for every tengu child who holds out *both* hands!" said Badger.

And each tengu child held out both hands, even the little child who was holding the fan. The magic nose fan dropped to the ground. Quickly, Badger grabbed it, tucked it into his belt, and ran away through the woods. Not one of the little tengu children got a sweet rice cake that day.

Badger walked and walked until he reached a city. Then he nosed around until he discovered the house of the wealthiest family in town. He pushed his way under the gate and into their yard. There he saw the family's beautiful young daughter, lying on the grass, taking a nap. Badger crept up to the place where the girl lay sleeping. She had the cutest little button nose. Badger slipped the magic nose fan from his belt, and he began to fan, and fan, and fan, and fan, and fan, and the girl's nose began to grow, and grow, and grow, and grow. Badger stopped fanning when her nose was just about six feet long. Then he put the fan back into his belt and waddled away.

When at last the girl awoke, and opened her eyes, she thought she saw something in the air, right above her face. She reached out to brush it away . . . *ouch!* It was her nose! She jumped up and ran to the house crying, "Mother, Father, Mother, Father, my nose, *my nose,* MY NOSE!"

The girl's mother and father didn't know what to do. First they locked the girl in her bedroom so that no one would see her. (She was just about the age to marry, and who would want a wife with such a long nose?) So they called in all the doctors of the town. The first doctor wrapped her nose in a poultice of herbs, but that only made it turn bright red. The second doctor pushed and poked her nose until it turned black and blue. The third wanted to give her a shot . . . in the nose! The girl screamed, and her parents sent the doctors away. Finally, her father was so desperate that he sent out a proclamation saying that whoever could cure his daughter's mysterious illness would receive her hand in marriage, and half his wealth in the bargain.

This was exactly what Badger had been waiting for. He changed himself into a rather good-looking young man and knocked on the rich man's door.

"I can cure your daughter," he said, "if you will allow me just two minutes alone with her."

The rich man agreed. He led Badger to the bedroom where his daughter lay sleeping.

Quickly, Badger took the fan from his belt, turned it over, and began to fan, and fan, and fan, and the girl's nose began to shrink, and shrink, and shrink, and finally all that remained was the cute little button nose she had had to begin with. And she was not at all unhappy when she saw her future husband, who was a rather good-looking young man. (That poor girl! She was about to marry a *badger,* and she didn't even know it.)

Badger was feeling very pleased with himself, and also rather tired. He strolled into the rich man's back yard, and stretched himself out on the grass. He closed his eyes and began to imagine all the things he would be able to buy with half the rich man's wealth. The sun shone hotter and hotter. Without thinking, Badger took the fan from his belt and began to fan, and fan, and fan, and fan. Badger's nose started to grow, and grow, and grow. It grew up through the leaves of the trees. It grew up through the clouds. It left the earth and went out into space. It grew all the way to the Milky Way.

Now, on that very day, a group of workers were building a bridge across the Milky Way. The bridge was made of logs, and it was almost finished. Just one more log was needed to complete the bridge. The workers were searching for the log they needed, when up through the clouds of the Milky Way, there appeared . . . Badger's nose. The workers grabbed the nose, tied it securely into the bridge, and went home for the day.

Back on Earth, a terrible pain woke Badger. He looked up and saw his nose disappearing through the clouds. Quickly, he turned the fan over and began desperately to fan, and fan, and fan, and fan, and his nose grew shorter, and shorter, and shorter, and shorter, but . . .

The end of Badger's nose was tied onto the bridge across the Milky Way; Badger's body was *not* tied to the Earth. Up shot Badger, through the clouds. He left the Earth and hurtled into space, across the Milky Way, to the bridge, where he dangled helplessly. He may still be dangling there today, I don't know. But I think he deserved it, don't you, for those mean tricks he played.

INTRODUCING THE STORY

Tengu and badgers are special creatures in Japanese tales. Children need to know a bit about them before hearing the story. We usually introduce it like this:

This story has two magical creatures in it, the tengu and the badger. Now, a tengu is a smallish sort of goblin with wings and a long nose. The tengu live in the forest, and they are almost never seen by human beings. It is said that they have special capes that make them invisible, so that people often hear them, but never see them.

A badger is a real animal, about the size of a raccoon, but not as cute. Badgers have pointed noses and short legs, and they waddle while they walk. They are nocturnal animals, which hunt by night and sleep in the daytime. In some of the stories from Japan, like this one, the badger is a magical animal, a troublemaker who can change into anything he wants. For instance, if a badger is being chased by a dog, he can change into a mouse [snap fingers] and scurry into a mousehole. In this story, he used his shape-changing powers to change into a human being.

TIPS FOR STORYTELLING

We like to tell this story using a real fan. It must, of course, have sides that are markedly different. The storyteller will need to practice using it before telling the story,so that one side is used consistently for *grow* and the other for *shrink*. When introducing Badger's ability to transform himself, we use a finger-snap. This same cue can be used later in the storytelling and in the creative dramatics activity involving transformation. A few simple mimes work well in telling this story, such as holding out one hand, then two, as the tengu children awaiting their rice cakes, or miming the astonished girl feeling her six-foot-long nose.

Participation Storytelling

Younger children will enjoy joining in any mimes the storyteller uses. It is also fun to add sound effects for the growing and shrinking noses. The children first practice making a rising "eee-eee" sound each time they hear the word *grow,* and a falling sound each time they hear the word *shrink.* The storyteller pauses after these words in the story, so that the audience may add the sound effects.

CREATIVE DRAMATICS

Nose Warm-ups

The leader fans the air with a real or imaginary nose fan, and the children feel their noses growing longer and longer, until they are three feet long.

Reach out and feel your nose. Your hand won't even reach the end of your three-foot-long nose. Now stand up and begin to walk around. Be careful not to touch anyone else with your nose. Now walk back to your place and sit down.

The leader now designates half the group as trees, who stand in a "forest" a full arm's length apart from each other on all sides. Trees stand still, arms at sides. The leader fans the noses of the remaining children again, which now grow to be *six feet long!* The children must weave their way in and out of the trees without bumping their imaginary noses into the trees or into anyone else. Walks in this warm-up activity work best when accompanied by a drumbeat.

Transformations

Children practice badger-like transformations. The leader calls out the name of an animal, snaps fingers, and the children twirl around. Coming out of the twirl, they freeze in the position of that animal. The leader can then use a drumbeat to "unfreeze" the animals and have them walk around the room as that animal might walk. Be sure to involve the group in deciding which animals to become. This activity may be extended into a guessing game in which individual children twirl and freeze into animal shapes of their own choice. Then the others guess the animal.

Scene Play

The leader divides the children into groups of seven to act out the scene in which the girl's parents call in the three doctors, and finally Badger comes and cures her long nose. Discuss the sequence of events as a large group, then let the smaller groups take over and work on planning and playing the scene simultaneously. One or more groups may want to share their scene with the others.

CREATIVE WRITING

Public Proclamation

The girl's father sent out a public proclamation, hoping to find someone to cure his daughter's nose. What did the proclamation look like? What did it say? What did he promise to the person who could cure his daughter's nose? Perhaps the proclamation had a picture of his daughter's long nose. Write the word "PROCLAMATION" across the top of a piece of paper, and begin.

A Letter from Badger

As Badger hung from the bridge over the Milky Way, an inhabitant of the area took pity on him and gave him a piece of paper and a pencil, an envelope and a stamp. Badger wrote a letter to a friend, describing what happened to him, telling how he felt as he hung from the bridge, and asking for help. Imagine that you are Badger, hanging from your nose from that bridge. This letter is your only chance to escape. You could begin your letter "Dear Uncle Badger," "Dear Best Friend Weasel," etc.

The Cloak of Invisibility

In some Japanese stories, the tengu possess another magical object besides a nose fan. They
wear cloaks that make them invisible. Write
another story about Badger in which he tricks a
tengu into giving him a cloak of invisibility.
What sort of mischief does Badger get into using
the cloak?

Buttercup

NORWAY

Once there lived a woman who had a son, a boy so round and fat, and so fond of good things to eat, that everyone called him Buttercup. The woman was in the kitchen one morning baking, and Buttercup sat at the table eating, when all at once the dog, Goldtooth, began to bark.

"Run outside, would you now, Buttercup, and see what Goldtooth is barking at."

So Buttercup ran out, and he came right back and said, "Oh heaven help us! Here comes a horrible troll with her head under her arm and a great big sack on her back."

"Get behind the breadboard, Buttercup, and hide, and don't you say a word."

Buttercup did as his mother told him. In came the old troll.

"Good day," said she.

"A good day to you, too," said Buttercup's mother.

"Isn't your Buttercup at home today?" asked the troll.

"No, he went out hunting with his father."

"Plague take it!" cried the troll. "I have the nicest little silver knife for him."

"Pip, pip, here I am." Up popped Buttercup.

"Oh, Buttercup, I have the nicest little silver knife for you, down in the bottom of my sack. But I am so old, and my back is so stiff, you must crawl in and fetch it yourself."

When Buttercup was well inside the bag, the troll threw it over her shoulder and strode off into the forest. And when they had gone a ways, the troll began to grow tired, and at last she set the sack down, and lay down next to it, and fell asleep. When Buttercup heard her snoring, he took the little silver knife and cut a hole in the sack. Then he crept out, and he put the heavy root of a pine tree into the sack in his place, and he ran off home to his mother.

When the troll got home to her house, and held the sack upside down, out fell the tree root on her foot, and she was furious.

The next day, Buttercup's mother was in the kitchen baking, and Buttercup sat at the table eating, and the dog, Goldtooth, began to bark.

"Run outside, Buttercup, my boy," said his mother, "and see what Goldtooth is barking at."

Buttercup ran outside, and twice as fast he was back inside.

"Heaven help us!" cried Buttercup. "If it isn't the old troll again, with her head under her arm, and a great sack on her back."

"Under the breadboard with you," said his mother, "and not a word out of you this time."

"Good day," said the troll. "Is your little Buttercup at home today?"

"I am sorry to say he is not," said his mother. "He is out in the woods, hunting with his father."

"Plague take it!" cried the troll. "I have the nicest little silver fork for him."

"Pip, pip, here I am." Up popped Buttercup.

"Oh, Buttercup, I am so old, and so stiff in the back," complained the troll. "You will have to climb down into my sack and get it yourself."

So, when Buttercup was well into the sack, the troll swung it over her shoulder and set off home as fast as her legs could carry her. But Buttercup was heavy, and she soon grew weary, and put down the sack, and lay down beside it, and fell asleep.

As soon as Buttercup heard the troll snoring, he poked a hole in the sack with the silver fork, and climbed out, and put a great huge stone inside in his place.

When the troll got home, she made a great fire on the hearth, and put a pot of water on, and got everything ready to boil Buttercup. But when she picked up the sack, and emptied it into the pot, the stone rolled out and broke the pot and splashed boiling water all over. Then the old troll was in a dreadful rage, and she said, "No matter how heavy Buttercup makes himself tomorrow, I shan't let him get away."

The next morning, Buttercup's mother was in the kitchen baking, and Buttercup sat at the table eating, and the dog, Goldtooth, began to bark.

"Do run outside, Buttercup, and see what Goldtooth is barking at."

Out he went, but soon he came back, crying, "Heaven save us! Here comes that old troll again, with her head under her arm and a sack on her back."

"Jump under the breadboard, Buttercup, and don't say a word."

"Good day," said the troll. "Is your Buttercup at home today?"

"You're very kind to ask after him," said Buttercup's mother, "but he is out in the woods hunting with his father."

"The plague take it!" said the troll. "Here I have such a beautiful little silver spoon for him."

"Pip, pip, here I am." Up popped Buttercup.

"Buttercup, I am so old, and my back is so stiff, you must creep into the sack and fetch the spoon yourself."

When Buttercup was well inside the sack, the troll swung it over her shoulder and set off as fast as she could. This time, she ran all the way to her house without stopping and threw the sack down on the table, and said to her daughter, "Take this, and make it into Buttercup broth." Then she set off to invite some other trolls, who were her friends, to dinner.

After the troll had gone out, the daughter (who was also a horrid troll) put her head down on the table and began to sob and cry.

"What's the matter?" asked Buttercup from inside the sack.

"My mother told me to make Buttercup broth, but I don't know how."

"Oh, that's simple," said Buttercup from inside the sack. "You make a fire, and you put a big kettle of water on to boil."

So she did.

"Now you put in some onions and some carrots and some cabbage."

So she did.

"Now you jump in, and pull the lid on after you."

So she did.

Buttercup crawled out of the sack, and he took the pine root and the great stone, and he carried them up onto the roof of the house. When the troll came back with all the other trolls, they thought they would just taste the broth. So one took a spoon, and sipped, and said,

"Good, by my troth,
Buttercup broth."

Buttercup put his head by the chimney and called down,

"Good, by my troth,
Troll's daughter broth."

"Who said that?" muttered the trolls. They looked all around the room, but they didn't see anyone. Then another troll took a spoon, and sipped, and said,

"Good, by my troth,
Buttercup broth."

Buttercup put his head by the chimney and called down, louder this time,

"Good, by my troth,
Troll's daughter broth."

"Who said that? Who said that?" The trolls looked in the corners of the room and under the beds, but they couldn't find anyone. Then the old troll herself sipped a spoonful from the pot and she said,

"Good, by my troth,
Buttercup broth."

Buttercup put his head by the chimney and called down in his loudest voice,

"Good, by my troth,
Troll's daughter broth."

The trolls rushed to the fireplace and looked up the chimney. Then Buttercup dropped the pine root and the great huge stone down on them and crushed them, and that was the end of the whole wicked lot of them, and they never carried off any more little children. Buttercup found a great box of gold and silver hidden by the hearth, and he brought it home to his mother. So of course they lived happily ever after.

INTRODUCING THE STORY

Most children will already know something about trolls from "The Three Billy Goats Gruff" or other Norwegian folktales, or even from J.R.R. Tolkien's *The Hobbit*. The storyteller can introduce "Buttercup" as a story about a boy and some trolls, and ask the children to share their recollections of what trolls are like. Like many monsters, they are large and cruel, but not very clever, and they are easily tricked by fast-thinking heroes and heroines. *D'Aulaire's Trolls,* by Ingri and Edgar Parin D'Aulaire, is a good source of information and stories about these imaginary creatures.

TIPS FOR STORYTELLING

We like to use an exaggerated, mock-sweet voice for the main troll; whenever she is foiled—by Buttercup's not being at home, or by the tricks he plays on her—she momentarily loses her sweet veneer, and her cruelty shows through in her voice. The troll's daughter should be portrayed as a blubbery, whining, and totally unsympathetic creature so that her demise in the cooking pot is not tragic. When Buttercup yells down the chimney to the trolls, his voice should be almost a whisper the first time, growing louder the second and third times.

Participation Storytelling

Younger children will want to hear this story more than once. On the second and subsequent tellings, have them rehearse and then join in as Buttercup saying, "Pip, pip, here I am," and as the trolls and Buttercup as they recite their rhymes beginning, "Good, by my troth . . ."

CREATIVE DRAMATICS

"Pip! Pip! Here I Am!"

This beginning drama activity can be performed with the children in seats or at desks. One or more children stand at their desks, or at a table, and play the role of Buttercup's mother. Other children may want to play the part of the dog, Goldtooth. The leader plays the part of the

old troll, and narrates as well. The children playing Buttercup crouch behind their chairs or desks, waiting for the troll
to say the line, "I have the nicest little silver knife [fork,
spoon] for him." Then they will jump up and say, "Pip! Pip!
Here I am." The leader can take this scene as far as the
children's concentration allows. When Buttercup crawls into
the troll's sack, all the children playing other characters may
wish to switch to the role of Buttercup.

Troll Walk

In a circle walk, or a random walk, the children
play the role of the troll. The leader beats out the troll's
heavy footsteps with the drum as she describes first the
hungry troll on her way to Buttercup's house, then the
happy troll carrying the heavy sack with Buttercup inside,
then the tired troll putting down her sack and falling asleep,
then the angry troll discovering the root in her sack.

Scene Play

The final scene can be played by groups of five or
more, beginning when the old troll tells her daughter to
make Buttercup broth. The leader narrates, pausing to give
the children an opportunity to improvise dialogue. Or,
groups may work independently of the leader.

CREATIVE WRITING

How Buttercup Found His Way Home

Use this map, which shows the path from But-
tercup's house to the troll's house, as a story-starter for the

children—either draw it onto the board, or give each child a copy of it.

> After Buttercup had defeated the trolls, and gotten their gold and silver, he had to find his way back home all by himself. He had traveled to the troll's house inside her sack, so he had no idea where he was . . . or did he? Buttercup was able to find his way back home because he had used senses other than sight to remember important things about the path from his house to the troll's. Write the story of how Buttercup found his way home, using the map to find clues.

Buttercup's Supper

> When Buttercup finally arrived home from the troll's house, carrying the great box of gold and silver, he was *very* hungry. His mother was so glad to see him that she cooked him every one of his favorite foods. Write a menu describing Buttercup's supper that night, remembering that in Buttercup's time there were no supermarkets. His mother made everything from scratch.

The Three Sillies

ENGLAND

Once upon a time there lived a farmer and his wife, and they had one daughter, and she was courted by a gentleman. Every evening he used to come and see her, and stay to supper at the farmhouse, and the daughter used to be sent down into the cellar to draw the beer for supper. So one evening she had gone down to draw the beer, and she happened to look up at the ceiling while she was drawing the beer, and up there she saw an axe stuck in one of the wooden beams. It must have been there a long time, but somehow or other she never noticed it before, and she began thinking. And she thought it was very dangerous to have that axe there, for, she said to herself, "Suppose he and I were to be married, and we were to have a son, and he were to grow up to be a man, and come down into the cellar to draw the beer, like I'm doing now, and the axe were to fall on his head and kill him, what a dreadful thing it would be!" And she put down the candle and the jug, and sat herself down and began crying.

Well, they began to wonder upstairs how it was that she was so long drawing the beer, and her mother went down to see after her, and she found her sitting on the bench crying, and the beer running all over the floor.

"Why, whatever is the matter?" said her mother.

"Oh, Mother!" says she. "Look at that horrid

axe. Suppose we were to be married, and were to have a son, and he were to grow up, and were to come down to the cellar to draw the beer, and the axe were to fall on his head and kill him, what a dreadful thing it would be."

"Dear, dear, what a dreadful thing it would be," said the mother, and she sat down beside the daughter and started crying too.

Then after a bit the father began to wonder that they didn't come back, and he went down into the cellar to look after them himself, and there they were sitting and crying, and the beer running all over the floor.

"Whatever is the matter?" says he.

"Why," says the mother, "look at that horrid axe up there. Just suppose, if our daughter and her sweetheart were to be married, and were to have a son, and he were to grow up, and were to come down into the cellar to draw beer, and the axe were to fall on his head and kill him, what a dreadful thing it would be."

"Dear, dear, dear, so it would," said the father, and he sat himself down beside the other two and started crying.

Now the gentleman got tired of waiting up in the kitchen by himself, and at last he went down into the cellar too, to see what they were about. There the three sat crying side by side, and the beer running all over the floor. And he ran straight and turned off the tap. Then he said, "Whatever are you three doing, sitting there crying, letting the beer run all over the floor?"

"Oh," says the father, "look at that horrid axe up there. Suppose you and our daughter were to be married, and were to have a son, and he were to grow up and were to come down into the cellar to draw the beer, and then the axe were to fall on his head and kill him." And then they started crying worse than before.

But the gentleman burst out laughing, and reached up and pulled out the axe, and then he said, "I've travelled many miles, and I never met three such big sillies as you three before. Now I shall start out on my travels again, and when I can find three bigger sillies than you three, then I'll come back and marry your daughter."

So he wished them good-bye, and started off on his travels, and left them all crying because the girl had lost her sweetheart.

Well, he set out, and he traveled a long way, and at last he came to a farm. And there the farmer was giving his hens boiling water to drink, and the hens would run away, and he would chase them back and try to get them to drink the boiling water again. So the gentleman asked the farmer what he was doing.

"I want my hens to lay hard-boiled eggs," the farmer answered.

Well, that was one big silly.

And the gentleman went on and on, and he went to an inn to stop for the night, and they were so full at the inn that they had to put him in a room with another traveller. The other man was a very pleasant fellow, and they got very friendly together. But in the morning, when they were both getting dressed, the gentleman was surprised to see the other hang his trousers on the knobs of the chest of drawers and run across the room full speed and leap into the air and try to land in the trousers. He tried over and over again, but he couldn't manage it. Finally the gentleman asked him what he was doing.

"Oh dear," says the man. "I do think trousers are the most awkwardest kind of clothes that ever were. I can't think who could have invented such things. It takes me the best part of an hour to get into mine every morning. How do you manage yours?"

So the gentleman burst out laughing, and showed him how to put them on, one leg at a time. The man was very much obliged to him, and said he never would have thought of doing it that way.

So that was the second big silly.

Then the gentleman went on his travels again, and he came to a village, and outside the village there was a pond, and round the pond was a crowd of people. And they had got rakes and brooms and pitchforks, and they were all reaching and poking them into the pond. The gentleman asked what was the matter.

"Why, matter enough!" they said. "Moon's tumbled into the pond, and we can't get her out!"

So the gentleman burst out laughing, and told them to look up into the sky, and that it was only the moon's reflection in the water. But they wouldn't listen to him, and abused him shamefully, and he got away as quick as he could.

So there was a whole lot of sillies bigger than those three sillies at home. The gentleman turned back home again and married the farmer's daughter, and if they didn't live happily for ever after, that's nothing to do with you and me.

INTRODUCING THE STORY

Children are always delighted to hear about people who know less than they do, and who do things they would never dream of doing. Most of the celebrated limericks of Edward Lear tell of such silly people; the rhyme and rhythm of his poetry make them all the more hilarious to young listeners. "The Three Sillies" can be introduced by three or more limericks such as:

> There was an Old Man of Peru,
> Who never knew what he should do;
> So he tore off his hair,
> And behaved like a bear,
> That intrinsic Old Man of Peru.

> There was an old man on the Border
> Who lived in the utmost disorder;
> He danced with the cat,
> And made tea in his hat,
> Which vexed all the folks on the Border.

> There was an old man with a beard,
> Who said, "It is just as I feared!—
> Two Owls and a Hen,
> Four larks and a Wren,
> Have all built their nests in my beard!"

TIPS FOR STORYTELLING

During the opening scene in the silly family's basement, younger children may need a cue from the storyteller that the characters are behaving foolishly. The storyteller might want to blubber in a ridiculous manner as the girl and her parents describe the improbable scenario of the as-yet-unborn son being killed by the falling axe.

CREATIVE DRAMATICS

Silly Walks

Silly walks make a good warm-up activity for dramatics based on "The Three Sillies." Some children may need guidance in inventing silly walks that are not chaotic. Using a drum for rhythm, the leader can narrate a "magnet walk." The children walk in a circle, and the leader walks in the circle with them. She tells them that she has a special magnet, a body magnet, that will pull on different parts of their bodies as they walk. It can change from a nose magnet, to a knee magnet, a back magnet (that makes them walk backwards), an elbow magnet—even a belly button magnet! The part of the body being pulled by the magnet will lead the rest of the body during the walk. The leader can also vary the rhythm of the drumbeat to speed up and slow down the walk and make it sillier.

A group of older children can be given several minutes to invent their own silly walks. Then one child demonstrates a walk, and the rest try to duplicate it.

Scene Play

The first two scenes in which the gentleman encounters the silly people can be acted out by small groups simultaneously as the leader narrates. Four or five children can act out the man trying to feed his hen boiling water, and pairs can play the scene where the gentleman teaches his roommate to put on his trousers correctly. Then, the whole group can act out the scene of the people trying to rescue the moon from the pond.

CREATIVE WRITING

"Have You Heard about the Sillies?"

Children love to invent other things that silly people do. This activity stimulates their imagination and also reinforces their feelings of competence. We give them the following framework for a poem:

Have you heard about the sillies?
Sillies_____,
Sillies_____,
Sillies_____,
Sillies_____,
But *I*_____.
Now you've heard about the Sillies,
And a little bit about me!

Three More Sillies

After the gentleman returned to the home of the three sillies, he married their daughter. Then he decided to take a job as a schoolteacher. And, would you believe it, on the first day of school, he saw three *more* sillies at school. The first silly . . .

How Anansi Got A Small Waist

WEST AFRICA

If you look closely at Anansi the spider, you will see that he has a fat head, and a thin, tiny waist, and a fat stomach. But it wasn't always so. Long ago, Anansi was one great, round blob. But then, one day, he got smaller in the middle. This is how it happened.

You see, Anansi liked nothing better than eating, and his favorite food was food that someone else had cooked for him. Anansi was especially fond of feasts—the kind that lasted half the day, where every sort of delicious food was served. Anansi's two favorite feasts were those that were held every year in Momojav, a village to the north of Anansi's, and in Kemojav, a village to the south. The ground-nut stew of the Momojav feast was famous throughout the country. The yams and cassava of Kemojav sent Anansi into a dance of ecstasy.

Now, it happened one year that the feasts at Momojav and at Kemojav were to take place on precisely the same day. When Anansi heard the news, he paced back and forth, stroking his whiskers, thinking, "How can I manage to eat at *both* feasts?"

Anansi traveled north to Momojav. He asked a man of the village, "At what time do you plan to begin the feast?"

"It will begin precisely," said the man, "when the food is ready."

Anansi traveled south to Kemojav. "When do you plan to begin serving food at your feast?" he asked a woman of the village. "When it is time," she replied.

Anansi walked home slowly. He was more determined than ever to eat at both feasts, so he sent his son Intikuma to borrow rope from everyone in the neighborhood. Then Anansi tied all the pieces of rope together, so that he had one very long rope.

When the feast day came, Anansi stood on the path, halfway between the villages of Momojav and Kemojav. He tied the center of that long, long rope around his middle. He gave one end of the rope to several of his children. "Go to Momojav," he ordered them. "When the feast begins, pull as hard as you can." He gave the other end of the rope to his other children. "Go to Kemojav," he told them. "When the people begin to eat, pull as hard as you can."

Anansi's children did as they were told. One group of little spiders went to Momojav carrying one end of the rope; the others went to Kemojav carrying the other end of the rope. Anansi stood on the path and waited.

Just by chance, the feast in Momojav and the feast in Kemojav began at exactly the same moment. Anansi's children in Momojav pulled on the rope, and Anansi took a big step toward the north. Then Anansi's children in Kemojav pulled on their end of the rope. Anansi turned around toward the south, but he found that he couldn't move. All of Anansi's children pulled hard, for a long time, without stopping. "Father will be angry with us if we don't pull as hard as we can," they said.

The rope grew tighter and tighter and tighter around Anansi's middle. The children began to wonder why their father did not come, so they dropped the rope and ran back to the place where they had left Anansi. They found their father lying helpless in the middle of the path. And he didn't look the same! Anansi's middle was as thin as a needle. The children lifted Anansi up and carried him home. He didn't feel like eating for a long time after that. And ever since then, Anansi has had a thin waist, all because he wanted to eat at two feasts on the same day.

INTRODUCING THE STORY

African riddles make good introductory material for African trickster tales. It takes children a while to become accustomed to these riddles, which are different from our contemporary American ones. They are not clever tricks with words, but rather clever ways of describing common objects and situations.

What is it you can see with one eye, but not with two?
The inside of a bottle.

It weighs less than a feather, yet no one wants to carry it.
A mosquito.

A boy dances, and puts a white hat on his head.
Popcorn.

For other African riddles, see *Ji-Nongo-Nongo Means Riddles* by Verna Aardema.

TIPS FOR STORYTELLING

This short, humorous story is easy to learn. The story could be deliciously embellished by a long description of authentic West African foods enthusiastically and mouthwateringly described by the storyteller; elaborate description of the clothing Anansi puts on to attend the feast could also be added. Such details, vividly evoked by the storyteller, add greatly to the enjoyment of the audience. They are best added by each individual teller as a result of his or her own research, tastes, and experience.

Participation Storytelling

Before telling the story, divide the audience into two sections. You needn't be too precise, just gesture toward an imaginary dividing line and those near the line can choose sides for themselves. The audience will play the part of Anansi's children during the story, so have them practice making the sound of spider children walking, drumming the fingers of one hand (flat fingers, not fingertips) on the palm of the other, and then rehearse pulling hard on an imaginary rope. Ask them to listen carefully to the story so they will know when to play their parts. During the telling, cue the walking noises and the rope pulling by an open-hand gesture to one or both groups.

CREATIVE DRAMATICS

Rope Tricks

As the group sits in a circle, the leader mimes picking up a long piece of imaginary rope, and tells the children that they will be passing the rope around the circle, and that each of them may do something with the rope. Some children may have original ideas, some may repeat what others have done. Children should show the weight and feel of the rope. The leader can discourage superficial playing by requesting that a child perform the mime again ("I didn't *see* that. Could you do it again more slowly?").

Two children mime turning an extraordinarily long jump rope. The other children jump in, one at a time, until all are jumping together. Timing group jumps without a real rope is a challenge!

Draw a chalk line across the floor, or lay down a long strip of masking tape to represent a tightrope, and let the children take turns crossing it in different ways: forwards, backwards, on one leg.

Divide into groups of four to six, and stage pantomime tugs-of-war.

Anansi, Before and After

As they walk in a circle, ask the group to show how Anansi looked before his waist was squeezed, and after. Working in pairs, have one child play Anansi, the other one of his children. How does Anansi accept a plate of food from his son or daughter before his waist was squeezed? After? How does he react when his son or daughter tells him about another feast—before his waist was squeezed? After?

Scene Play

This story is short and may be easily acted out from start to finish. It offers sufficient roles for a group of twenty or more children. First retell the story as a group and recall what the characters said and did. Then decide on the geography of the playing space; locate Anansi's house, Momojav, Kemojav, and the path that connects the two towns. The leader may choose to play the part of Anansi in order to keep control of a less experienced group, or may designate a child to play the role. The remaining children should be divided into four groups: two groups of spider children, plus the residents of Momojav and Kemojav. These groups are then given a few minutes to discuss what they will be doing during the play: preparing for the feast, cooking, cleaning house, dressing, etc. When all are ready, they take their places, and one of Anansi's children begins the drama by telling him that the feasts of Momojav and Kemojav are to be held on the same day. After playing the story through, discuss what changes might need to be made, and replay it with the same or different casting.

CREATIVE WRITING

Comic Strip

Choose your favorite scene from the story, and draw a sequence of two or three pictures telling what happened in that scene. Write the words or the thoughts of the characters in the scene in cartoon "bubbles" above their heads.

Children may have difficulty choosing one scene or part of the story to illustrate. The group can brainstorm a list of good ideas for comic strip art.

What If . . .

Imagine that the following year, the feasts at Momojav and at Kemojav were *again* held on the same day. This time, Anansi is more determined than ever to discover a way to eat at both feasts. How will he do this? Will his children help him? Will he be successful, or will he once again fail, or even cause harm to himself?

Jack and the Beanstalk

ENGLAND

There was once upon a time a poor widow who had an only son named Jack, and a cow named Milky-White. And all they had to live on was the milk the cow gave every morning which they carried to the market and sold. But one morning Milky-White gave no milk and they didn't know what to do.

"What shall we do, what shall we do?" said the widow, wringing her hands.

"Cheer up, Mother, I'll go and get work somewhere," said Jack.

"We tried that before, and no one would have you," said his mother. "No, we must sell Milky-White, and with the money set up shop or something."

"All right, Mother," says Jack. "It's market day today, and I'll soon sell Milky-White, and then we'll see what we can do."

So he took the cow's halter in his hand, and off he started. He hadn't gone far when he met a funny-looking old man who said to him, "Good morning, Jack."

"Good morning to you," said Jack, and wondered how the man knew his name.

"Well, Jack, and where are you off to?" said the man.

"I'm going to market to sell our cow here."

"Oh, you look the proper sort of chap to sell cows," said the man. "I wonder if you know how many beans make five."

"Two in each hand and one in your mouth," says Jack, as sharp as a needle.

"Right you are," says the man, "and here they are, the very beans themselves," he went on, pulling out of his pocket a number of strange-looking beans. "As you are so sharp," says he, "I don't mind doing a swap with you—your cow for these beans."

"Go on," says Jack, "wouldn't you like it?"

"Ah! You don't know what these beans are," said the man. "If you plant them at night, by morning they grow right up to the sky."

"Really?" says Jack. "You don't say."

"Yes, that is so, and if it doesn't turn out to be true, you can have your cow back."

"Right," says Jack, and hands him over Milky-White's halter and pockets the beans.

Back home goes Jack, and as he hadn't gone very far, it wasn't dusk by the time he got to his door.

"Back already, Jack?" said his mother. "I see you haven't got Milky-White, so you've sold her. How much did you get for her?"

"You'll never guess, Mother," says Jack.

"Good boy! Five pounds, ten, fifteen? No, it can't be twenty!"

"I told you you couldn't guess. What do you say to these beans? They're magical. Plant them at night and . . ."

"What!" says Jack's mother. "Have you been such a fool, such a dolt, such an idiot, as to give away my Milky-White, the best milker in the parish, and prime beef to boot, for a set of paltry beans. Take that! Take that! Take that! And as for your precious beans, here they go out the window. And now, off to bed with you, and not a sup shall you drink and not a bite shall you swallow this very night."

So Jack went upstairs to his little room in the attic, and sad and sorry he was, to be sure, as much for his mother's sake as for the loss of his supper.

At last he dropped off to sleep. When he woke up, the room looked so funny. The sun was shining into part of it, and yet all the rest was quite dark and shady. So Jack jumped up and dressed himself and went to the window. And what do you think he saw? Why, the beans his mother had thrown out of the window into the garden had sprung up into a big beanstalk which went up and up and up till it reached the sky. So the man spoke truth after all.

The beanstalk grew up quite close to Jack's window, so all he had to do was to open it and give a jump on to the beanstalk which ran up just like a big ladder. So Jack climbed, and he climbed, and he climbed and he climbed and he climbed until at last he reached the sky. And when he got there, he found a long broad road going as straight as a dart. So he walked along and he walked along and he walked along till he came to a great big house, and on the doorstep there stood a great big tall woman.

"Good morning, mum," says Jack, quite polite-like. "Could you be so kind as to give me some breakfast?" For he hadn't had anything to eat, you know, the night before, and was as hungry as a hunter.

"It's breakfast you want, is it?" says the great big tall woman. "It's breakfast you'll *be* if you don't move off from here, for my man is an ogre, and there's nothing he likes better for breakfast than boys broiled on toast."

"Oh, please, do give me something to eat, mum. I've had nothing to eat since yesterday morning, really and truly, mum," says Jack. "I may as well be broiled as to die of hunger."

Well, the ogre's wife was not half so bad after all. She took Jack into the kitchen, and gave him a chunk of bread and a jug of milk. But Jack had only just begun to eat when—thump! thump! thump!—the whole house shook with the sound of someone coming.

"Goodness gracious me! It's my old man," said the ogre's wife. "What on earth shall I do? Come along quick and jump in here." And she bundled Jack into the oven just as the ogre came in.

He was a big one, to be sure. From his belt hung three calves, and he unhooked them and threw them down on the table and said, "Here, wife, broil me a couple of these for breakfast. But wait. What's this I smell?

> Fee-fi-fo-fum,
> I smell the blood of an Englishman,
> Be he live or be he dead,
> I'll grind his bones to make my bread!"

"Nonsense, dear," said his wife, "you're dreaming. Or perhaps you smell the scraps of that little boy you liked so much for yesterday's dinner. You go and have a wash and tidy up, and by the time you come back, your breakfast'll be ready for you."

So off the ogre went, and Jack was just going to jump out of the oven and run away when the woman told him no. "Wait until he's asleep," says she. "He always has a doze after breakfast."

Well, the ogre had his breakfast, and after that he goes to a big chest and takes out of it a couple of bags of gold, and down he sits and counts till at last his head began to nod, and he began to snore like thunder.

Then Jack crept out on tiptoe from the oven, and as he was passing the ogre, he took one of the bags of gold under his arm, and off he pelters till he came to the beanstalk, and then he threw down the bag of gold, which fell right into his mother's garden, of course. And then he climbed down and climbed down till at last he got home, and showed his mother the gold and said, "Well, Mother, wasn't I right about the beans? They are really magical, you see."

They lived on the gold for some time, but at last they came to the end of it, and Jack made up his mind to try his luck once more up at the top of the beanstalk. So one fine morning he rose up early and got to the beanstalk, and he climbed and he climbed till at last he came out on the same road as before, and walked up to the great big house. There, sure enough, was the great big tall woman standing on the doorstep.

"Good morning, mum," says Jack, as bold as brass. "Could you be so good as to give me something to eat?"

"Go away, my boy," said the big tall woman, "or else my man will eat you up for breakfast. But aren't you the youngster who came here once before? Do you know, that very day, my man missed one of his bags of gold."

"That's strange, mum," says Jack, "I daresay I could tell you something about that, but I'm so hungry I can't speak till I've had something to eat."

Well the big tall woman was so curious that she took him in and gave him something to eat. But he had scarcely begun munching it as slowly as he could when— thump! thump! thump!—they heard the ogre's footsteps, and his wife hid Jack away in the oven.

All happened as it did before. In came the ogre as he did before, said,

"Fee-fi-fo-fum,
I smell the blood of an Englishman,
Be he live or be he dead,
I'll grind his bones to make my bread!"

and he had his breakfast of three broiled oxen. Then he said, "Wife, bring one of the hens that lays the golden eggs." So she brought it, and the ogre said, "Lay," and it laid an egg all of gold. And then the ogre began to nod his head, and to snore till the house shook.

Then Jack crept out of the oven on tiptoe and caught hold of the golden hen, and was off before you could say "Jack Robinson." But this time the hen gave a cackle which woke the ogre, and just as Jack got out of the house he heard him calling, "Wife, wife, what have you done with my golden hen?"

And the wife said, "Why, my dear?"

But that was all Jack heard, for he rushed off to the beanstalk and climbed down like a house on fire. And when he got home he showed his mother the wonderful hen and said "Lay," to it, and it laid a golden egg every time he said "Lay."

Well, Jack was not content, and it wasn't very long before he determined to have another try at his luck up there at the top of the beanstalk. So one fine morning, he rose up early, and got on to the beanstalk, and he climbed and he climbed and he climbed and he climbed till he got to the top. But this time he knew better than to go straight to the ogre's house. And when he got near it he waited behind a bush till he saw the ogre's wife come out with a pail to get some water, and then he crept into the house and got into the copper kettle. He hadn't been there long when he heard—thump! thump! thump!—as before, and in came the ogre and his wife.

> "Fee-fi-fo-fum,
> I smell the blood of an Englishman!
> Be he live or be he dead,
> I'll grind his bones to make my bread!"

cried the ogre. "I smell him, wife, I smell him."

"Do you, my dearie?" said the ogre's wife. "Then if it's that little rogue that stole your gold and your hen, he's sure to have got into the oven." And they both rushed to the oven. But Jack wasn't there, luckily, and the ogre's wife said, "There you go again with your fee-fi-fo-fum. Why, you'll just be smelling the boy you caught last night. Imagine you not knowing the difference between live and dead after all these years."

So the ogre sat down to the breakfast and ate it, and after the breakfast was over, the ogre called out, "Wife, bring me my golden harp." So she brought it and put it on the table before him. Then he said, "Sing!" and the golden harp sang most beautifully. And it went on singing till the ogre fell asleep, and commenced to snore like thunder.

Then Jack lifted up the copper lid very quietly and got down like a mouse and crept on hands and knees till he came to the table. Then up he crawled and caught hold of the golden harp and dashed with it towards the door. But the harp called out quite loud, "Master! Master!" and the ogre woke up just in time to see Jack running off with his harp.

Jack ran as fast as he could, and the ogre came rushing after, and would soon have caught him, only Jack had a start and dodged him a bit, and knew where he was going. When he got to the beanstalk, the ogre was not more than twenty yards away when suddenly he saw Jack disappear like, and when he came to the end of the road, he saw Jack below, climbing down for dear life. Well, the ogre didn't like trusting himself to such a ladder, and he stood and waited, so Jack got another start. But just then the harp cried out, "Master! Master!" and the ogre swung himself down onto the beanstalk which shook with his weight. Down climbs Jack, and after him climbed the ogre. By this time Jack had climbed down and climbed down and climbed down till he was very nearly home. So he called out, "Mother! Mother! Bring me an axe! Bring me an axe!" And his mother came rushing out with the axe in her hand, but when she came to the beanstalk, she stood stock still with fright, for there she saw the ogre with his legs just through the clouds.

But Jack jumped down and got hold of the axe and gave a chop at the beanstalk, and cut it half in two. The ogre felt the beanstalk shake and quiver so he stopped to see what was the matter. Then Jack gave another chop with the axe, and the beanstalk was cut in two and began to topple over. Then the ogre fell down and broke his crown, and the beanstalk came toppling after.

Then Jack showed his mother his golden harp, and what with showing that and selling the golden eggs, Jack and his mother became very rich, and he married a great princess, and they lived happily ever after.

INTRODUCING THE STORY

We like to begin telling well-known stories without announcing the title. Children might resist listening to a story they *think* they already know. They have probably never heard this particular version of "Jack and the Beanstalk," with its unique language. Older children may consider this story beneath their level of maturity; however, a promise of creative dramatics and creative writing activities to follow motivates them to listen attentively.

TIPS FOR STORYTELLING

This version of "Jack and the Beanstalk," first published by Joseph Jacobs in the 1890s, is long, but the familiarity of the basic story and the repetition make it fairly easy to learn. The rhythmic flow of the language, and the charming expressions throughout, make it a delight to tell.

Participation Storytelling

Participation will make it easier for younger children to listen attentively to this longish story. Introduce the ogre's chant (fee-fi-fo-fum), and have the children repeat it several times. Then describe the ogre's great size and his bad temper. Have the children practice saying the chant again, this time as a great, huge, mean ogre would. The chant occurs three times in the story; cue the audience to join in with a pause and an expectant look.

CREATIVE DRAMATICS

Imaginary Objects

The group sits in a circle, and the leader talks about some of the objects in the story, then mimes picking each one up and carefully passing it to the child next to her. Each object is passed around the entire circle. Pass the magic beans, the cup that Jack drank from at the ogre's house, the bag of gold, the hen that laid the golden egg, and the golden harp. Ask children to think of any other objects to pass.

Giant Walk

The villain of this story is referred to as an ogre, though in other versions he is called a giant. In either case, he is very large. Pretending to be a giant is a creative dramatics activity that never fails to capture children's imaginations.

The children walk in a circle, or at random, as giants. As they walk, the leader narrates activities such as crossing a mountain range in a few steps, wading across the ocean, drinking up lakes, walking across a burning desert, and so on. "Good" giants can rescue people who are drowning and put them in their pocket, blow out forest fires like candles on a birthday cake, plug up volcanoes, or wrestle down tornadoes. Children will also want to add their own ideas to the giant walk.

Ogre's House

Everything in the ogre's house was much too large for Jack. The leader narrates as the children mime being Jack in the ogre's house: climbing up the tall front steps, getting up into a chair, drinking milk from an enormous glass, using a huge knife to butter a piece of bread that is half as big as he is.

Scene Play

Children in groups of three—Jack, man, and Mother—plan and then act out three scenes: Jack's mother sending him to market, Jack trading their cow to the man for the magic beans, and Jack telling his mother about the beans and being sent to bed without any supper.

CREATIVE WRITING

Magic Beans

This activity involves creating a "seed packet" for Jack's magic beans. After the beanstalk fell, suppose that Jack discovered hundreds of beans lying on the ground all around it. He decided to dry them, put them in packages, and sell them. The children will probably need to examine real seed packets, observing what type of illustrations are used and what kind of information is printed on the package. Should Jack's magic beans have a warning label? Children can use envelopes for this project, or make their own. Large dried beans can be colored with markers to make the magic beans.

Ogre's Diary

Usually the ogre wrote the same thing in his diary every day: "Ate three calves" or "Had another young chap for breakfast this morning." But on the very first day that Jack visited him, he wrote in his diary,
"Dear Diary,
The oddest things happened this morning . . ."

A Different Beanstalk Adventure

Suppose Jack had had one more adventure at the top of the beanstalk . . . that once, he decided not to go to the ogre's house, but instead to see what lay in the opposite direction. The leader can use guided imagery to begin:

Even though he already had the hen that laid the golden eggs, Jack decided that he would have another try at the top of the beanstalk. He grabbed onto the beanstalk and he climbed up

and up and up until he came to that same land.
Off in the distance, he could see the ogre's house,
but Jack decided to go in the opposite direction.
There was a road leading off through the clouds,
and Jack began to run along, and run along . . .

Baba Yaga

RUSSIA

Once upon a time there lived a man whose wife had died, leaving him with two children—twins—a boy and a girl. The three of them lived quite happily together, until the man took a notion to marry again. Now, usually when a father takes a new wife, he chooses a kind woman who will care for his children as if they were her own. But such was not the case for the twins. Their new mother found fault with everything they did. Their manners at table were disgusting, she said, and they had to eat in the corner. She gave them only hard, dry crusts of bread. Still, she said, she couldn't bear to watch them eat, so she sent them outside. And that was in Russia, in the wintertime.

One day the woman called the twins inside. "It is such a bother having you two about the house, I am sending you to live with my granny. Just follow the forest trail," she said, "and you will come to her hut. You will recognize it because it stands up off the ground on chicken legs."

So the children set out together, and the little girl (who had heard stories about the hut on chicken legs) said that they should go first to visit their own grandmother, and ask for her advice.

When their grandmother heard where they were going, she cried out, "Oh, you poor children. That woman is not sending you to live with her grandmother, but with Baba Yaga, the bony-legged, the witch. And yet, you are both kind and good children. There is a chance that you can escape from her." Then she gave them a loaf of bread and a piece of meat and a jar of milk. To the girl she gave a comb and a hair-ribbon, and to the boy she gave a small, round mirror. "You may find a use for these," she said, and she kissed them good-bye.

The two children followed the path which led into the dark and gloomy wood. Finally they reached a clearing, and there they saw it, the hut on chicken legs. Slowly they walked toward it. But in order to get into the yard, they had to make their way through a thick tangle of birch trees. The trees were so bent that their branches almost touched the ground.

"You poor trees," said the girl, and she used her hair-ribbon to tie up their branches. Then she and her brother passed through, into the yard of the hut.

All of a sudden, a huge dog came running toward them. It had an enormous head, and its jaws were wide open, ready to swallow the two children. The boy took the piece of meat and threw it straight into the dog's mouth. The great beast lay down, and chewed on the meat, and wagged its tail happily.

Then the children climbed the ladder that led to the door of the hut, and knocked softly.

"Come in."

Slowly they opened the door. There she was, Baba Yaga, the bony-legged, the witch. She lay on the floor with her head near the door, one foot in one corner of the hut, one foot in the other corner, and her knees nearly touching the ceiling. Her hair hung down about her face like coils of snakes. When she spoke, her iron teeth crashed together and made a sound like thunder and shot off sparks of lightning.

"Good morning, granny," said the boy. "Our stepmother has sent us to stay with you."

"Good. You shall wait on me and serve me, but if you cannot do the jobs I give you, I shall have to put you in a pan and fry you in the oven, my pretty darlings."

So she set the girl down at a loom and told her to weave a piece of cloth by sundown. To the boy she gave a sieve, and told him to go fetch water from the well. Then she went off into the woods. But from time to time she came striding back, and stood under the window of the hut, and called out,

"Are you weaving, my pet?
Are you weaving, my pretty?"

And the girl would answer, "Yes, granny, I am weaving."

The boy tried and tried to take water up from the well in the sieve, but the water just ran out the holes. So he sat down by the edge of the well and began to cry. Just then, a flock of birds landed beside him, and he remembered his bread. He took the loaf, and broke off little pieces, and gave them to the birds. Then the birds flew off, and each one returned with a bit of soft clay in its beak. They put the clay into all the holes of the sieve, so that it would hold water, and the boy was able to carry the water back to the hut.

The girl sat by the loom, weaving as fast as she could, "clack, clack, clackity-clack," but she knew she could never weave a whole piece of cloth by sundown. Baba Yaga came to the window and called out,

"Are you weaving, my pet?
Are you weaving, my pretty?"

The girl answered, "I am weaving, granny." Then she felt something warm against her foot. It was the very thinnest cat she had ever seen.

"Poor kitty," said the girl. "Here, have some of our milk." She poured a saucer full, which the cat drank. Then the cat sat up on her back legs and spoke: "You are good children, and you must run away as fast as you can. I shall sit and weave for you, so that Baba Yaga will not know that you are gone. Run!"

The boy and the girl hurried out the door of the hut and climbed down the ladder. They ran past the dog, past the birch trees, and down the forest path.

Baba Yaga came to the window and called out,

"Are you weaving, my pet?
Are you weaving, my pretty?"

And the cat answered, "Meow!"

Baba Yaga flew into the house, and when she saw that the children were gone, she grabbed the cat by the neck and cried out, "Why didn't you claw their eyes out?"

"In all the years that I have served you," said the cat, "you never even gave me a saucer of water to drink. Those nice children gave me sweet milk."

Baba Yaga ran out into the yard, grabbed the dog by the ears and cried, "Why didn't you tear them to pieces?"

"In all the years that I have served you," said the dog, "you never even gave me an old dried-up bone. Those nice children gave me a piece of fresh meat."

Baba Yaga seized the birch trees and cried, "Why didn't you grab them in your branches?"

"In all the years that we have served you," said the birch trees, "you never even tied us up with old twine. Those nice children used this pretty ribbon."

Baba Yaga raced back to her hut, jumped in her mortar and grabbed her pestle and her broom, and set off down the path. In her mortar, she travelled faster than the wind, and the children soon heard the sound of the pestle beating against the ground:

Thump, thump, thumpity-thump,
Thump, thump, thumpity-thump.

The girl reached in her pocket and threw the little comb behind her, and from the spot where it landed, there grew up a forest, and the trees of that forest were so close together that Baba Yaga could not pass through. She had to go around, and that took a long time. The children ran on, but before they could get home, they again heard the sound of Baba Yaga's pestle beating against the ground:

Thump, thump, thumpity-thump,
Thump, thump, thumpity-thump.

Now the boy reached in his pocket and took out the mirror and threw it behind him. From the spot where it landed, there sprang up a wide, rushing river. When Baba Yaga reached the shore of that river, she stopped. She couldn't cross the water. (*You* know what happens when a witch touches water!) So Baba Yaga had to turn around and go back to her little hut on chicken legs.

When the children reached their own house, they told their father everything that had happened, and he sent that cruel woman away forever. And after that, he and the two children lived very happily ever after.

INTRODUCING THE STORY

Many tales from Russia tell of Baba Yaga, the witch. She has so many unique and unexpected qualities, we like to describe her, her house, and her mortar and pestle to the children before they hear the story.

Baba Yaga lives in a little house in the forest that stands up on four chicken legs, and she can make the house move by saying the magic words, "Izbushka, Izbushka." Baba Yaga is very tall and very thin. Her long stringy hair looks like it is made out of snakes, and her iron teeth send off sparks like lightning when she talks. Baba Yaga doesn't travel on a broom, like some witches do, but in a big bowl called a mortar, and she pushes herself along with a big stick called a pestle, and uses a broom in her other hand to sweep away her tracks.

Sometimes, we tell the audience what Baba Yaga likes best for her supper (little children), or what the fence around her hut is made out of (human bones), but we follow this by saying that we are all very lucky that she lived so far away, and such a long, long time ago.

TIPS FOR STORYTELLING

The boy and girl in the story are given six helpful or magic objects by their grandmother. As we reach the point in the story where they are about to use each one, we slow down and pause just an instant, so that the audience can have the pleasure of guessing which one they will use. When the twins use the last object, the mirror, we often ask the audience to tell us which object is left. The audience will join in spontaneously on the "clack, clack, clackity-clack" of the loom, and on the "thump, thump, thumpity-thump" of Baba Yaga travelling in her mortar and pestle.

CREATIVE DRAMATICS

Warm-ups

Children can mime character actions suggested by the leader and by the group members, such as the twins sitting out in the cold with only hard crusts of bread to eat, or Baba Yaga travelling in her mortar and pestle, sweeping away her tracks with the broom. Pairs of children holding hands can play Baba Yaga's hut, responding to the leader's commands, such as, "Izbushka, Izbushka, turn around . . . move to the east . . . move to the west . . . walk through the woods . . . bend down so I can see inside . . ."

Group Sculpture

The leader has the group describe Baba Yaga as she looks when the twins first see her, lying on the floor of her hut. They then make a group sculpture of Baba Yaga. Depending upon the size of the group, children can be her long, bony arms and legs, her jaws, her snaky hair. Once the group is satisfied with the sculpture, experiment with having her talk and move parts of her body. The machine warm–up, described in the Creative Dramatics chapter, can be done before this activity, and will help the children conceptualize the group sculpture.

The giant Baba Yaga sculpture could be an attraction at a carnival or amusement park; the leader, playing the role of the carnival barker, gives a tour of the Baba Yaga, telling imaginary spectators various facts about her. Children especially enjoy this kind of "talking up" of their creative dramatics projects by the leader.

Scene Play

"Baba Yaga" contains many good, short, two– and three–person scenes that can be acted out by small groups simultaneously. Also, the leader can divide the story into scenes and play it out in its entirety, changing the cast with each new scene.

The final chase scene can be played by the whole group, with the twins running in place at one side of the playing space and Baba Yaga rumbling along in place in her mortar at the other side. All the other children lie flat on the floor between them, and when the story narration comes to the point where the children throw the comb behind them, these children spring up and become the forest. After Baba Yaga finds her way around the forest, the children again lay on the floor between Baba Yaga and the twins, waiting for their cue to become the raging river.

CREATIVE WRITING

"I Know a Witch . . ."

Write a poem telling everything you know about Baba Yaga, following this form,

> I know a witch named Baba Yaga.
> Baba Yaga has iron teeth,
> Baba Yaga_____,
> Baba Yaga_____,
> (etc.)

With a group of younger children, the leader may wish to write these words on the chalkboard, or to give each child a sheet of paper that has the words printed on it. The lines of the poems don't necessarily need to rhyme.

Older children can write a poem of rhymed couplets. The first line of each couplet can tell a fact that everyone knows about Baba Yaga, and the second line can be some new fact the child has invented, for example:

> Baba Yaga's house is on chicken legs,
> Baba Yaga likes to eat raw eggs . . .

Letters to an Advice Columnist

Taking the point of view of one of the characters in "Baba Yaga," children write letters to Dear Abby or Ann Landers, describing their problems and asking for advice. Children then switch letters with one another and respond.

How Fire Came to Earth

NORTHWEST COAST INDIAN

Long, long ago, when the animals lived on the earth like people, there was no fire. Everyone was miserable and cold. They gathered together to keep warm and to cheer each other up.

One day, Eagle spoke up and said, "I have seen fire in the homes of the sky people." Eagle was able to fly higher than any other creature. Raven complained that *he* couldn't fly that high, and had never seen fire, and didn't know what Eagle was talking about. "Let's shoot arrows, and make a bridge up to the sky," said Eagle.

Raven tried to shoot arrows into the sky, but failed. Wolf, Caribou, Beaver, Woodpecker, Spider, and Frog all tried, but they failed also. No one could shoot an arrow as high as the sky. Then, tiny Chickadee stepped forward and said, "Let me try." All the animals laughed at Chickadee. Raven, who laughed loudest, said, "You are too little to shoot the sky. Your bow is bigger than you are." He laughed and laughed.

Chickadee pulled back his bowstring and aimed his arrow. The arrow shot up and up, and it stuck in the sky. He shot another arrow, and that one stuck into the end of the first. He shot another arrow, and that one stuck into the end of the second. He used up all his arrows, then he used Raven's arrows, then Caribou's, then Wolf's. He used everyone's arrows, and when he was done, he had made an arrow bridge to the sky.

Eagle said to Bear, "You stay here on the ground and guard the bridge." Bear grumbled, but he agreed. Then all the animals walked up the arrow bridge to the sky. They saw the houses of the sky people. Smoke was pouring out of the holes in their roofs. They began sneaking up on the houses of the sky people.

Beaver said he would get the fire. He lay down in front of the door of one of the houses and pretended to be dead. An old woman of the sky people found him and said, "Look at this strange creature." She took Beaver into the house and began to cut off his fur, saying, "This will make a nice hat and mittens for my husband." Beaver bit a piece of his fur. As long as he had a piece of fur in his mouth, he could not be killed.

Outside the house, the animal people were becoming impatient. Woodpecker flew to a tree and began to tap, rat-a-tat, rat-a-tat, rat-a-tat. The sky people ran out to see what that sound was. The old woman and her husband stared at woodpecker. She said, "That creature is pounding his head into the tree." The old man said, "Such a little head. Such a loud noise."

While the sky people stared at Woodpecker, Beaver rolled himself onto his skin and put his fur back on. He grabbed a flaming stick from the fire-pit and ran out the door. Beaver scurried behind the sky people, but they saw him and ran along after him. When Beaver became tired of running, he passed the fire to Wolf. Eagle flew above the runners. He screeched and yelled, telling them to go faster, that the sky people were gaining on them.

Meanwhile, on the ground, Bear was beginning to worry, "All my friends who went to the sky must be hungry now. I will take food to them." Bear loaded a pack with food. Bear was huge and his pack of food was heavy. He was too much for the bridge. Under the weight of Bear and his load, the arrow bridge broke. Bear tumbled and crashed to the ground. He got up, roared with anger, and lumbered away. That fall made Bear mean and angry; to this day, he is still mean.

In the sky land, the animals kept running with the fire. They ran all the way to the edge of the sky land, but when they got there, they saw that their bridge was gone. The sky people were getting closer. Eagle, Raven, and Woodpecker could fly down, but the others would be trapped. Spider said, "I will make a basket and lower each one of you down." She lowered all of the animals. Last was Frog, who held the flaming stick in his mouth.

The sky people looked down and saw frog holding the fire. They began to make rain, first a light rain, then a heavy rain. Frog jumped out of the basket and tumbled to the ground, where he fell in a thicket of bushes. The other animal people saw him fall, and they began to cry, "Surely the fire has gone out."

Out jumped Frog from the thick tangle of bushes and said, "I saved some sparks of fire from the rain, and I hid them in the brush."

Eagle and Wolf gathered up some sticks. They began to rub and twirl them together. The wood became hot, it began to smoke, then it burst into flame.

Eagle was the first to feel the warmth of the fire, and he said, "This is good. Frog has hidden the fire. Now, whenever we want fire, we will find it inside the wood." The animal people rejoiced. They gathered around the fire and ate, and sang, and danced.

INTRODUCING THE STORY

Many Native American stories tell of an early time when animals lived on Earth like people. Although they participated in all sorts of human activities, these first people had animal powers also, related to their species. Eagle could fly, for example, and the skunk had a powerful odor-weapon. "How Fire Came to Earth" is a composite of stories from several Northwest Coast tribes.

TIPS FOR STORYTELLING

The storyteller must keep in mind that the characters in this tale are respected ancestor figures, not cute, fuzzy animals. Imagine the physical appearance and personality of each one. When you recount the story, you will want to remember it as if you were there. Recall the oppressive cold, the fearful flight from the sky people, and the joy that everyone felt when the fire was discovered inside the wood. Visualize the earth and sky, creating a vivid landscape that will make the story come alive for you, and thus for your audience.

Participation Storytelling

This story can be retold with members of the audience providing sound effects. Some possibilities are:

claves (wood blocks)	animals' teeth chattering from cold woodpecker pecking tree
slide whistle up	arrows flying to the sky
slide whistle down	arrow bridge falling
drum	bear falling on the ground footsteps of the sky people
tambourine or maracas	rain falling
sandpaper blocks	rubbing sticks together for fire woman cutting beaver's fur

CREATIVE DRAMATICS

Warm-ups

As the children sit in a circle, the leader narrates a scenario in which the children imagine they are getting colder and colder. It is winter, the wind begins to blow, the snow starts falling, the sun sets . . . In turn, the children show ways in which they could keep warm, *other* than starting a fire.

Then, the group mimes gathering wood, builds an imaginary fire, and huddles around its warmth. The children can share ideas of what they would like to do now that they are gathered around the fire and are finally warm. Have they ever sat around a campfire? What kinds of things do people do around a fire? These activities can be mimed by the group.

To the beat of a drum, have the children walk as the various animal characters in the story and as the supernatural sky people. Decide together how the sky people will move. End the warm-up session with an activity that children particularly enjoy—taking arrows from a quiver, loading a bow, and shooting arrows to the sky.

Scene Play

In playing the sky scene, the leader divides the group into sky people and animal people. Each group decides what they will be doing as the scene opens—sky people will be going about their daily life, animal people will be planning how to get the fire from them. In order to make the chase scene manageable, have the group play it out in slow motion, running back and forth across the playing space. When the animal people reach the place where they left the arrow ladder, the sky people run in place until spider lowers the other animal people to earth in her basket.

A final scene replays the campfire warm-up activity, but with the children in character as animals this time. They can dance, as animals, to the beat of the leader's drum.

CREATIVE WRITING

One Animal's Story

The group recalls names of the various animal characters in the story, and the leader lists their names on the board. Then each child chooses a character and writes a story for that animal's grandchildren and great-grandchildren, telling about the important role he played in bringing fire to the people of the Earth.

Fire Under the Sea

Another Northwest Coast tale tells of fire being kept by the people who live under the sea.

One day, a piece of charred wood floated up to the surface of the ocean. It was still hot when the animal people found it. Then they realized that someone living at the bottom of the sea must have fire! Write a story telling how the animal people manage to get the fire from them. What were the people called who had the fire? Which animals went after it? How did they bring it up to dry land?

Taily-po

Once there was an old man who lived all by himself in a one-room cabin in the woods, down in Tennessee. And that one room was his bedroom, his living room, his dining room, and his kitchen, all rolled up in one.

One day, the old man went out hunting with his hound dogs. Their names were Uno, and Ino, and Cumptico-Calico. The whole day long, they didn't see a living thing in the woods—not a possum, not a rabbit, not even a squirrel. Everything was so quiet and still. Not even the wind was out in the woods that day.

So when the old man got home, he didn't have any food to cook for his supper. But he built up the fire in the fireplace, and he put a pot of water on for coffee, and he sat back in his rocking chair and waited for the water to boil.

All of a sudden, the front door opened up and in rushed a great big hairy thing, and it raced around and around and around the room. The man jumped up and he grabbed his axe and swung at that thing. Chopped off its tail. Then that thing howled and shot out the door, and those hound dogs—Uno, and Ino, and Cumptico-Calico—lit out after it.

Well, the old man looked at the tail. It was long

and skinny, like a possum's, but it was all covered with thick hairs like wires. He looked at it, and he said, "Well, it's better than nothing." So he dropped it in that boiling water, cooked it, and ate it.

By that time, those hound dogs came back moping and whining and laid down under the front porch. The man locked the front door, and covered up the fire, and blew out the candles, got into bed, and pulled the covers up under his chin.

Then he heard a noise, outside, on the wall of the cabin,

Scratch,
scratch,
scratch,

And a voice that said,

"Taily-po,
Taily-po,
I'm coming to get my taily-po!"

The man sat up in his bed and he called out to his hound dogs,

"Uno!
Ino!
Cumptico-Calico!"

And those dogs came running out from under the front porch, chased that mean old ugly thing back into the swamp.

Then the old man lay back down, and he pulled the covers up, and he closed his eyes, but he couldn't seem to get to sleep. After awhile, he heard a sound. It was on the front door this time.

Scratch,
scratch,
scratch.

Then he heard a voice, said,

"Taily-po,
Taily-po,
All I want is my taily-po!"

The man set up in bed and he yelled for his hound dogs,

"Uno!
Ino!
Cumptico-Calico!"

And the dogs came running out from under the front porch, chased that mean old ugly thing back into the swamp. But that thing led those dogs around and around the swamp and it *lost* them. They didn't come back.

The old man lay back down in his bed and pulled the covers up over his head and tried to go to sleep. But pretty soon he heard a rustling noise near a place where there was a crack in his cabin wall. Then he heard,

Scratch,
scratch,
scratch.

Only this time, the scratching was right on the
foot of the old man's bed. The old man pulled the covers off
his face and looked. He saw two pointy ears. Underneath the
two pointy ears were two big round eyes. Underneath the
two big round eyes was a mouth full of long pointy teeth.

"Taily-po!
Taily-po!
You know and I know
THAT YOU'VE GOT MY TAILY-PO!"

The man sat up and called out for his dogs,

"Uno!
Ino!
Cumptico-Calico!"

Nothing. He called again, with all his power,

"Uno!
Ino!
Cumptico-Calico!"

But those dogs didn't come, 'cause they weren't
there. They were down in the swamp, lost.

Now, if you should go out by those woods, in
Tennessee, you might see something tall and straight. Looks

like a tree with no branches. It's the stone chimney . . . all that's left of that old man's cabin. And if you should happen to wander down by the swamp, you might hear a noise, sounds like some howling. Sounds like some hound dogs. Sounds like . . . Uno . . . and Ino . . . and Cumptico-Calico. And you might hear something else, sounds like the wind. Sounds like,

> "Taily-po!
> Taily-po!
> Now I've GOT my Taily-po!"

INTRODUCING THE STORY

Of all the stories we tell, this is the one that children most often request to hear again and again. Its scariness is relieved by the repetition of humorous words, and it is deliciously frightening but at the same time a bit ridiculous. The storyteller can introduce this story by talking about scary stories in general. When and where do people usually tell scary stories? What are some of the frightening and mysterious settings in which the stories are said to have taken place?

TIPS FOR STORYTELLING

A slow, serious, deliberate telling allows the audience to relish the suspense of this tale. Take time to develop the listeners' mental image of the man's cabin. Scary stories are enhanced by minute realistic detail. Pause frequently, as if you are trying to remember all the significant events of the story. Give the ending softly and slowly, then, in a loud voice, "Now I've GOT my Taily-po!" Despite the repetition of lines, this is *not* a story for audience participation. Whenever children join in on the "scratch, scratch, scratch," others inevitably hush them.

CREATIVE DRAMATICS

A Walk in the Swamp

In a circle walk or random walk, the children pretend to be the man in the story, walking in the woods. The leader narrates, describing the changing and challenging environment the man has to walk through: tall grass, thick thorn bushes, sticky swamp mud . . . maybe even quicksand! Pause from time to time and listen to the stillness of the swamp.

Taily-po Monster

The leader narrates as the children simultaneously play the part of the monster.

It is late evening in the swamp, and you are just waking up. Feel the mud all around you. What sounds do you hear? You begin to feel hungry, so you decide to take a swim in the river. You walk down to the water. Do you walk on two legs, or four legs? You wade deeper and deeper into the water; now you are swimming. You decide to dive down to find some supper. Decide what you want to eat. Now dive down, grab it, and eat it. Now you swim to the mud, and you walk up out of the water. Get the mud and water out of your fur. You look all around, and you see a light in the distance. It is coming from the man's cabin. You walk slowly toward the light . . .

Scene Play

The leader narrates as all the children mime the actions of the man after he returns home from hunting in the evening.

Then the children work independently of the leader in small groups. In groups of five, children play the scene of the man going to bed for the first time, the monster coming, and the dogs chasing the monster back to the swamp. The leader moves from group to group, offering advice if the children are having trouble deciding how to play the scene.

This tale is short enough to be easily acted out in its entirety. The group sits in a circle; the leader narrates, changing the cast at the beginning of each scene, so that children alternate playing and observing. The leader lets the children take as much control as possible of the action and dialogue of the story.

CREATIVE WRITING

Beware the Taily-po

> After the mysterious disappearance of the old man who lived in the cabin in the woods, along with his three dogs, a park ranger heard rumors about the Taily-po monster. The ranger decided to make a poster warning hikers, hunters, and fishermen about the dangerous creature living down in the swamp. Make a warning poster: write "BEWARE THE TAILY-PO" at the top of a piece of paper. Underneath, draw a picture of what you think the monster looked like, and at the bottom give a description of the monster's evil deeds and describe any warning signs that the monster has been in the area.

What if . . .

> Uno, Ino, and Cumptico-Calico lived on for many years after the old man disappeared. Tell the story of what happened to them. Did they stay together, or were they separated? Did they find new homes?

The Angry Stories

KOREA

Once upon a time there lived a boy, the son of a wealthy family, who loved nothing in the world so much as to listen to stories. Whenever he met a stranger, he would ask to be told a story, until he had heard hundreds and thousands of stories. But he would never tell these stories to anyone else. Instead, he kept them stuffed inside a leather bag which he hung on a hook in his closet. He kept the leather bag closed tight, and never ever let the stories out.

The boy eventually grew to be a handsome young man, and the time came for him to marry. His family arranged for him to wed a lovely young woman who lived about a day's journey away. Everyone in the household set to work preparing for the wedding, including the old servant who was especially fond of the young man. This servant was preparing his master's clothes for the journey, when he heard some strange mutterings and murmurings. The noises seemed to come from the closet. The servant searched and found the leather bag, the one the young man had used to hide away all the stories he had heard in his childhood. The old man listened carefully.

"Pay attention, everyone," said a small voice, "the boy's wedding is to take place tomorrow. All these years he has kept us prisoners in this tiny bag. We have suffered too long. We should pay him back for this mistreatment."

"Yes," said another tiny voice, "I have been thinking the same thing. Tomorrow he will leave to travel to his bride's house. I shall change into a patch of bright red strawberries growing by the side of the road. I shall be poisonous, but I shall look so delicious that he will want to eat me. When he does, he will become deathly ill."

"If that doesn't work," chimed in a third small voice, "I shall become a clear, bubbling spring by the roadside. I shall have a gourd dipper floating on my surface. When he sees me, he will feel thirsty and will drink me. Then he will suffer!"

The servant heard a fourth voice. "If you fail, then I shall become a red hot iron poker. I will hide in the bag of rice chaff that will be placed by his horse when he dismounts at the bride's house. And when he steps on me, I shall burn his feet."

A fifth voice whispered, "And I shall become a poisonous snake, and I shall hide in the bridal chamber, and when the bride and bridegroom have gone to sleep, I shall come out and bite them."

The servant was terrified by what he heard. The spirits of the stories must be very powerful, and they were so angry at his young master. He resolved to lead the young man's horse all the way to the bride's house, and to prevent these evil deeds from taking place.

Early the next morning, the wedding procession stood ready to leave the house. The groom, handsomely dressed in his best clothes, came out of the house and mounted his horse. Suddenly, the faithful servant ran outside, stood beside the horse, and asked to be allowed to lead the procession.

The young man's father said, "You have other work to do. You are very old. You will become tired."

"I must lead the young master's horse today, I insist," said the servant. Finally the young man consented, and allowed the servant to lead his horse to the bride's home.

The procession marched along, and passed by a forest. Among the trees, within sight of the road, grew a patch of large, red strawberries.

"Stop," cried the young bridegroom. "I must have those strawberries. Stop at once."

The servant would not stop, but he only prodded the horse to walk faster, saying, "Those berries are not good. We will find sweeter ones later."

In the heat of the day, they came to a bubbling spring by the roadside. Its water looked cool and refreshing to the travelers, and there was even a gourd dipper floating on the water, inviting them to drink.

"Bring me a dipper of that water," the bridegroom commanded his servant. "I am quite thirsty."

Again, the servant prodded the horse to go faster and hurried away. "That water is not good," he said. "You will quench your thirst when we reach our destination." The bridegroom was becoming angry and impatient, but the servant marched on without looking back. Finally, they reached the home of the bride. A great crowd had gathered in the yard, and a bag of rice chaff had been set out for the young man to dismount upon. The servant stopped the horse beside the bag of chaff, but just as the bridegroom was about to dismount, the servant pretended to fall, and knocked his master to the ground, well out of the way of the rice chaff. The young man blushed in shame at his clumsy arrival. Secretly he was very angry at the servant. He walked silently into the house.

When night fell, the bride and bridegroom retired to their bedchamber. The servant armed himself with a sword and hid on the balcony, just outside their room. As soon as the bride and bridegroom went to bed, the servant jumped in through the window and ordered them to get up. He pulled back the covers and lifted the mattress. There lay a poisonous snake, coiled and ready to bite. The servant cut off the snake's head with one blow. Then he sighed, and sat down, and began to tell his master the story of the voices he had heard, coming from the old leather bag.

The next morning, the bag of rice chaff was found burned and charred, with the iron poker inside. Everyone thanked the old servant, and congratulated him on his courage. As for the young man, he realized that he could not be greedy and hide away the stories he heard. Stories are meant to be shared and passed on to others.

INTRODUCING THE STORY

This is a tale about—among other things—the importance of storytelling. The storyteller may introduce "The Angry Stories" by talking about the art of storytelling, and particularly about the words we use to let people know that we are about to tell a story that is make-believe. Most children know the formula "once upon a time." One very

funny opening formula comes from Joseph Jacobs' version
of "The Story of the Three Little Pigs":

> Once upon a time, when pigs spoke rhyme,
> And monkeys chewed tobacco,
> And hens took snuff to make them tough,
> And ducks said 'quack-o, quack-o' . . .

Stories from Turkey and Armenia often begin

> Once there was and once there wasn't . . .

Perhaps some children, whose parents speak
another language, know other story openings they can teach
the group. For more examples of traditional story openings
and closings, see Anne Pellowski's *The World of Storytelling.*

TIPS FOR STORYTELLING

A mental map of the boy's route, and of the
bride's house, is very helpful in telling the story. If the
storyteller has clearly visualized the dangers the boy will
face, it will be easy to remember them and the order in
which they will appear when the stories are talking inside the
bag. We give the stories funny, nasty little voices, ones that
are menacing but also slightly amusing.

CREATIVE DRAMATICS

Warm-ups

Children make believe they are the stories in the
story bag. They move to the center of the circle and push

inwards, as the leader coaches them to talk about how they can't move, can't breathe, etc. Then they return to their places and transform slowly, to a drumbeat, first into the poison strawberries, then the cool spring, the red hot poker, and last, the snake. Most of these transformations will be *felt* by the individual children much more than they will be visually recognizable to an observer. This identification and empathy is one of the main goals of creative dramatics. The leader needs to recognize the level of a child's concentration through facial expression as well as quality of movement.

Interview

The leader selects some students to play the bag: they join hands and encircle a group of "stories." Each child who is playing a story in the bag decides exactly which story he is. The leader plays the role of a reporter. With a real or imaginary microphone, he or she interviews the "stories," asking their name (title), how long they have been in the bag, how they feel about it, and if and how they are planning revenge on the young man.

Story Charades

"The Angry Stories" provides a chance for children to act out scenes from some well-known and favorite stories. Groups of three or four decide on a story and practice a one minute pantomime of it. They perform the mime for the group, which watches silently until the minute has elapsed and guesses are asked for by the leader. Younger groups will probably need to use dialogue in their charades; advanced groups should use pantomime only.

CREATIVE WRITING

Group Story Creation

Small groups of children sit in a circle or around a table. Each child begins a story, writing two sentences on a sheet of paper, and then passes the story to the right. The next person reads those two sentences and writes two more sentences, and so on. Three-part stories, by three writers, are good to start with, emphasizing beginning, middle, and end. Later, the groups may choose to write longer stories. Each group chooses the group story creation they like best to be read aloud.

Briar Rose

GERMANY

Once upon a time, there lived a queen and a king who wanted more than anything in the world to have a child. One day, when the queen was bathing in the river, a frog crept out of the water onto the land, and said to her, "Your wish shall be fulfilled. Before a year has gone by, you will have a daughter."

The frog's words came true. The queen gave birth to a little girl who was so beautiful that the king could hardly contain his joy. He planned a great celebration at the palace, inviting all his kin and friends and acquaintances. He did not forget to invite the wise women of the kingdom, for his baby daughter would need their blessing. Now, in his kingdom, there lived thirteen wise women, but the king had only twelve golden plates with which to serve them. For fear of offending one of them, he only invited twelve.

The celebration was held, and everyone ate and drank to their heart's content. Then, one by one, the wise women bestowed their magical gifts upon the baby. One gave her the gift of wisdom, another gave her the gift of kindness, another gave her the gift of beauty, and so on. But just after the eleventh wise woman had spoken, suddenly there appeared at the door to the banquet hall the thirteenth wise woman, the one who had not been invited. She rushed in, without greeting or even looking at any of the guests, and cried in a loud voice, "The king's daughter shall in her fifteenth year cut herself on a spindle and fall down dead." And without saying another word, she turned and left the room.

All the guests sat for a long time in silence. Then up spoke the twelfth wise woman, the one who had not yet bestowed her gifts upon the child.

"I cannot change this evil spell, I can only soften it," she said. "The girl will not die, but only fall into a deep sleep of a hundred years."

The king and the queen gave orders that every spindle in the whole kingdom should immediately be burnt. Meanwhile the gifts of the wise women were fulfilled. The girl grew to be good-natured, wise, and beautiful, and everyone who knew her loved her.

It happened that on the very day when she was fifteen years old, the king and queen were not at home, and the girl was left alone in the palace. She went and looked into all the rooms and bedchambers just as she pleased, and at last she came to an old tower. She climbed up the narrow winding staircase and found a little door. A rusty key was in the lock, and when she turned it the door sprang open. There sat an old, old woman, spinning flax with a spindle.

"Good day," said the girl. "What are you doing?" She had never seen anyone spin before, since all the spindles in the kingdom had been destroyed.

"I am spinning, my dear," said the old woman, nodding her head.

"May I try?" the girl asked. But scarcely had she touched the spindle when the magic decree was fulfilled, and she cut her finger on it.

At that very moment, she collapsed upon the bed that stood there, and fell into a deep sleep. And this sleep extended over the whole palace; the king and the queen, who had just come home, and had entered the great hall, began to go to sleep, and the whole of the court with them. The horses in the stable went to sleep, and the dogs in the yard, and the pigeons on the roof. Even the flies on the wall went to sleep. The fire that was flaming on the hearth became quiet and slept. The cook, who was just about to pull the hair of the scullery boy, because he had forgotten something, let go of him and went to sleep. The wind fell quiet and a great stillness was everywhere.

Around the palace, there began to grow a hedge of thorns, which every year became higher and higher, until at last it covered everything. Nothing could be seen of the palace, not even the flags upon the high turrets. The story of the beautiful sleeping princess, Briar Rose, began to spread throughout the whole country. From time to time, kings' sons came and tried to get through the thorny hedge into the castle. But they found it impossible, for the thorns held fast together, as if they had hands, and the youths were caught in them, and could not get loose again.

After many, many years a king's son came again to that country and heard an old man talking about the thorn hedge, and how a palace was said to stand behind it in which a wonderfully beautiful princess had been asleep for a hundred years.

The youth was seized with a desire to see the sleeping princess, and although the old man sought to dissuade him, he would not listen.

The youth approached the thorn hedge just as the hundred years was up, and the time had come when Briar

Rose was to awaken again. As he walked nearer, the thorns turned one by one to beautiful flowers, which parted from each other of their own accord and let him pass through unhurt. In the palace yard he saw the horses and the spotted hounds lying asleep. On the roof the pigeons slept with their heads under their wings. Inside, the flies were asleep on the wall, and the king and queen slept on their thrones.

The youth went further, and all was so quiet he could hear his own breath. At last he came to the tower, and opened the door into the little room where Briar Rose lay sleeping. He stooped down to look at her more closely, and at that moment she opened her eyes, and circled her arms around him, and they kissed.

Then they went together into the great hall. The king and queen and all their courtiers were just waking up. The horses in the courtyard stood up and shook themselves; the hounds jumped up and wagged their tails. The pigeons on the roof pulled their heads from under their wings and flew off. The flies on the wall crept again, the fire in the kitchen burned again, and the cook gave the scullery boy such a box on the ear that he screamed.

The marriage of the king's son with Briar Rose was celebrated with great splendor, and they lived contented the rest of their days.

INTRODUCING THE STORY

"Briar Rose" is a variant of the tale "Sleeping Beauty," but here, the title and text are from the collection of the Brothers Grimm, rather than Charles Perrault's

French tales. We find that using the title "Briar Rose" minimizes the group's expectations that they will be hearing the Disney version.

"Briar Rose" is a special kind of folktale, a fairy tale. A fairy tale is different from other folktales because it deals with "coming of age." The hero or heroine is a child, living with his or her parents, at the beginning of the story. By the end of the fairy tale, there has been a wedding, and a promise of "happily ever after." By the age of nine or ten, children are ready not only to appreciate fairy tales (that begins around age five), but also to begin to make comparisons between them and to form ideas about typical structure and contents. A telling of "Briar Rose" could begin with a group discussion of spells and enchantments in fairy tales: Who uses them? Upon whom they are used? How are they broken? "The Frog Prince" is a well-known example of a fairy tale with an enchantment, as is "Snow White."

TIPS FOR STORYTELLING

"Briar Rose" is a tale that relies on description, rather than dialogue or action, for most of its unfolding. The storyteller needs to visualize the layout of the palace and to memorize its inhabitants and the order in which they doze off. The portrayal of the people and animals in the palace, how they fall asleep, and how they wake up, provides the storyteller an opportunity to add her own personal touches to the tale; this is basically a comic interlude, and can be changed, as long as any added details seem medieval.

CREATIVE DRAMATICS

Scene Play: Hundred Years' Sleep

Designate portions of the playing space as the various parts of the castle: throne room, kitchen, courtyard, stables. Some of the children go to each area, and they decide what activity they will be performing. Repetitive sorts of action such as sewing, hammering, stirring the soup, brushing the horses, or pitching hay are best for this activity. The leader begins a drumbeat, and all begin acting as the inhabitants of the castle. The drumbeats begin to get slower and slower, and all motions slow accordingly until everyone freezes in the position they held at the last drumbeat. Try to hold the freeze almost to the children's limit, then begin beating the drum, picking up the tempo until everyone is performing their activities as they were at the beginning of the scene.

Scene Play: Christening

The christening scene requires about twenty-five or thirty children, playing the roles of king, queen, baby, thirteen wise women, other guests, and servants. It can be played at tables, or sitting on the floor. With a scene this complex, a group planning session of five minutes or so will be needed before playing begins. The children need to decide on the seating arrangement, what types of food and drink are being served, and when and how the thirteen wise women will make their entrances. Are the wise women young or old? The first eleven wise women will have to decide upon gifts to bestow upon the little princess, and announce them during the scene.

The leader provides narration and pacing, while the children supply action and dialogue. With the narrative, the leader tries to evoke the sudden mood change brought about by the entrance and pronouncement of the thirteenth wise woman, and then the relief that is felt when the twelfth is able to partially undo the curse. The scene can end with the king and queen sending the servants and guests out to find and burn all the spindles in the kingdom.

Scene Play: Hedge of Thorns

A circle of children, crouched on the ground, grow up slowly, arms interwoven, into the hedge of thorns. Another child plays the role of the old man who advises the princes to go away, and several children can play the princes who become caught in the hedge. As the last prince approaches the hedge, the leader can begin a drumbeat and narration of the transformation of the briars to beautiful flowers. A romantically inclined group may wish to have a sleeping princess at the center of the vines.

CREATIVE WRITING

Gifts of the Wise Women

What are some "gifts" that a baby should receive, gifts that are not bought in a store? Can you list eleven that would make life more interesting? More fun? More satisfying? Recall the gifts mentioned in the story. See also the beginning of "The Three Golden Hairs of Grandfather Know-It-All," the last story in this book, for other magical gifts to newborn babies.

Extra! Extra!

Briar Rose awakening from a hundred-years' sleep is news! The group can brainstorm suitable headlines, and write news articles describing the event, which should include a dateline, a condensed summary of the facts, and details of an interview with Briar Rose, her parents, or the prince. Fifth and sixth graders have found this activity highly enjoyable. Their productions were not very serious, of course, but an older group often enjoys parodying a story they have heard many times.

The Sprightly Tailor

SCOTLAND

A sprightly tailor was employed by the great laird, Macdonald, in his castle at Saddell, in order to make the laird a pair of trews, used in olden time. And trews—being the vest and trousers united in one piece, and ornamented with fringes—were very comfortable, and suitable to be worn in walking or dancing. And Macdonald said to the tailor that if he would make the trews by night in the church, he would get a handsome reward. For it was thought that the old ruined church was haunted, and that fearsome things were to be seen there at night.

The tailor was well aware of this; but he was a sprightly man, and when the laird dared him to make the trews by night in the church, the tailor was not to be daunted, but took it in hand to gain the prize. So, when night came, away he went up the glen, about half a mile distant from the castle, till he came to the old church. Then he chose him a nice flat gravestone for a seat and he lighted his candle, and put on his thimble, and set to work making the trews, plying his needle nimbly, and thinking about the reward that the laird would have to give him.

For some time he got on pretty well, until he felt the ground all of a tremble under his feet; and looking about him, but keeping his fingers at work, he saw the appearance of a great human head rising up through the stone pavement of the church. And when the head had risen above the surface, there came from it a great, great voice. And the voice said, "Do you see this big head of mine?"

"I see that, but I'll sew this!" replied the sprightly tailor; and he stitched away at the trews.

Then the head rose higher up through the pavement, until its neck appeared. And when its neck was shown, the thundering voice came again and said, "Do you see this great big neck of mine?"

"I see that, but I'll sew this!" said the sprightly tailor; and he stitched away at his trews.

Then the head and neck rose higher still, until the great shoulders and chest were shown above the ground. And again the mighty voice thundered, "Do you see this great big chest of mine?"

And again the sprightly tailor replied, "I see that, but I'll sew this!" And he stitched away at his trews.

And still it kept rising through the pavement, until it shook a great pair of arms in the tailor's face, and said, "Do you see these great big arms of mine?"

"I see those, but I'll sew this!" answered the tailor, and he stitched hard at his trews, for he knew that he had no time to lose.

The sprightly tailor was taking the long stitches, when he saw it slowly rising and rising through the floor, until it lifted out a great leg, and stamping with it upon the pavement, said in a roaring voice, "Do you see this great big leg of mine?"

"Aye, aye. I see that, but I'll sew this!" cried the tailor, and his fingers flew with the needle, and he took such long stitches that he was just coming to the end of the trews when it was bringing up its other great leg. But before it could pull the leg out of the ground, the sprightly tailor had finished his task, and, blowing out his candle, and springing from off his gravestone, he buckled up, and ran out of the church with the trews under his arm. Then the fearsome thing gave a loud roar, and stamped with both his feet upon the pavement, and out of the church he went after the sprightly tailor.

Down the glen they ran, faster than the stream when the flood rides it. But the tailor had got the start and a nimble pair of legs, and he did not choose to lose Macdonald's reward. And though the thing roared at him to stop, yet the sprightly tailor was not the man to listen to such a monster. So he held his trews tight, and let no darkness grow under his feet, until he had reached Saddell Castle. He had no sooner got inside the gate, and shut it, than the monster came up to it. And, enraged at losing the tailor, it struck the stone wall above the gate with its five great fingers. You may see them plainly to this day, if you'll only look close enough.

The sprightly tailor gained his reward, for Macdonald paid him handsomely for the trews, and never discovered that a few of the stitches were somewhat l o n g.

INTRODUCING THE STORY

The marks that the monster leaves on the castle wall offer "proof" that this story is true. The storyteller may wish to begin the story by describing the marks on the wall, or even drawing a picture of them. "The Sprightly Tailor" is one of many stories about a person who willingly goes into a dangerous place—on a dare, on a bet, or out of foolishness. The sprightly tailor agrees to spend the night in the haunted churchyard in return for a reward. A discussion of why people take dares and bets can precede the storytelling.

The storyteller may wish to say that the events in this story took place on Halloween night.

TIPS FOR STORYTELLING

The language in this tale is essential to its effect, and the storyteller should keep as close to the written text as possible. The teller will need to choose a way to portray the character of the monster. This could be a change of voice—a low, raspy voice, or even a hoarse, whispery voice work well—or just a change of tempo, facial expression, or body position. The portrayal of the monster should contrast with that of the tailor's "sprightly" personality. The story can be told slowly and menacingly, picking up in pace after the tailor begins to run.

CREATIVE DRAWINGS

Warm-ups

The children imagine they are the monster as the leader narrates,

> You are deep, deep, under the ground. It's dark. You can feel the weight of the earth and rocks on each part of your body. You can't move. Suddenly, from far away, you hear the church bell as it begins to ring twelve times. Very slowly, you

push your head up out of the earth, then your right
arm, then your left arm. Now push! Lift your
body out. Now your right leg. Pull hard. Now
your left leg. Now stand up. You're free! Take
some steps. [Begin to walk in a circle to a drumbeat.]

Frightening Walk

Using a drum to beat out a varying tempo of
footsteps, the leader narrates a circle walk or random walk
through scary places that are suggested by the children: near
the haunted house, into a cave, through the woods at night.
Turn the lights down low.

Scene Play

The scene in the churchyard, with the tailor
sewing and the monster slowly emerging from the ground,
may be acted out by pairs of children, half playing the role of
the monster, the other half the part of the tailor. In a room
with tables, tailors can sit cross-legged on tables while
monsters crouch behind them, emerging over the tabletops
during the story. The leader narrates, and the group recites
the dialogue from the story.

CREATIVE WRITING

Excellent Trews!

Write an advertisement for trews. Draw a picture
of them from the description in the story: "being

the vest and trousers united in one piece, and ornamented with fringes . . . very comfortable, and suitable to be worn in walking or dancing." What color would they be? What pattern? Be sure to include the price, the tailor's name and address, and perhaps quotes from satisfied customers. How about a guarantee? Would people be more likely to buy the trews if they knew they were made by the famous tailor who escaped the monster in the churchyard?

Write an Urban Legend

When working in schools, we often give students the story-starter entitled "The Bent Tetherball Pole." Most children know what a tetherball pole is like: a very strong metal pipe which could not easily be bent. We make up the beginning of a story that happened, perhaps at a nearby school, in which the students came to school one day and found that the tetherball pole had been bent in the shape of a pretzel (well, almost), and we draw a simple picture of it. We then ask the children to write a legend telling how the pole was bent. Some of the stories will have supernatural elements, and some will not, depending on the children. It is best to give them the option of providing either a supernatural or a scientific explanation.

Coyote, Iktome, and the Rock

SIOUX INDIAN

Coyote was walking with his friend, Iktome. Along their path stood Iya, the rock. This was not just any rock; it was special. It had those spidery lines of green moss all over it, the kind that tell a story. Iya had power.

Coyote said, "Why, this is a nice-looking rock. I think it has power." Coyote took off the thick blanket he was wearing and put it on the rock. "Here, Iya, take this as a present. Take this blanket, friend rock, to keep you from freezing. You must feel cold."

"Wow, a giveaway!" said Iktome. "You sure are in a giving mood today, friend."

"Ah, it's nothing, I'm always giving things away. Iya looks real nice in my blanket."

"His blanket now," said Iktome.

The two friends went on. Pretty soon a cold rain started. The rain turned to hail. The hail turned to slush. Coyote and Iktome took refuge in a cave, which was cold and wet. Iktome was all right; he had his thick buffalo robe. Coyote had only his shirt, and he was shivering. He was freezing. His teeth were chattering.

"*Kola,* friend of mine," Coyote said to Iktome, "go back and get me my fine blanket. I need it, and that rock has no use for it. He's been getting along without a blanket for ages. Hurry; I'm freezing!"

Iktome went back to Iya, saying, "Can I have that blanket back, please?"

The rock said, "No, I like it. What is given is given."

Iktome returned and told Coyote, "He won't give it back."

"That no-good, ungrateful rock!" said Coyote. "Has he paid for the blanket? Has he worked for it? I'll go get it myself."

"Friend," said Iktome, "Tunka, Iya, the rock—there's a lot of power there! Maybe you should let him keep it."

"Are you crazy? This is an expensive blanket of many colors and great thickness. I'll go talk to him."

Coyote went back and told Iya, "Hey, rock! What's the meaning of this? What do you need a blanket for? Let me have it back right now!"

"No," said the rock, "what is given is given."

"You're a bad rock! Don't you care that I'm freezing to death? That I'll catch a cold?" Coyote jerked the blanket away from Iya and put it on. "So there; that's the end of it."

"By no means the end," said the rock.

Coyote went back to the cave. The rain and hail had stopped and the sun came out again, so Coyote and Iktome sat before the cave, sunning themselves, eating pemmican and fry-bread and *wojapi,* berry soup. After eating, they took out their pipes and had a smoke.

All of a sudden Iktome said, "What's that noise?"

"What noise? I don't hear anything."

"A crashing, a rumble far off."

"Yes, friend, I hear it now."

"Friend Coyote, it's getting stronger and nearer, like thunder or an earthquake."

"It is rather strong and loud. I wonder what it can be."

"I have a pretty good idea, friend," said Iktome.

Then they saw the great rock. It was Iya, rolling, thundering, crashing upon them.

"Friend, let's run for it!" cried Iktome. "Iya means to kills us!"

The two ran as fast as they could while the rock rolled after them, coming closer and closer.

"Friend, let's swim the river. The rock is so heavy, he surely can't swim!" cried Iktome. So they swam the river, but Iya, the great rock, also swam over the river as if it had been made of wood.

"Friend, into the timber, among the big trees," cried Coyote. "That big rock surely can't get through this thick forest." They ran among the trees, but the huge Iya came rolling along after them, shivering and splintering the big pines to pieces, left and right.

The two came out onto the flats. "Oh! Oh!" cried Iktome, Spider Man. "Friend Coyote, this is really not my quarrel. I just remembered, I have pressing business to attend to. So long!" Iktome rolled himself into a tiny ball and became a spider. He disappeared into a mousehole.

Coyote ran on and on, the big rock thundering close at his heels. Then Iya, the big rock, rolled right over Coyote, flattening him out altogether.

Iya took the blanket and rolled back to his own place, saying, "So there!"

A *wasichu* rancher riding along saw Coyote lying there all flattened out. "What a nice rug!" said the rancher, picking Coyote up, and he took the rug home.

The rancher put Coyote right in front of his fireplace. Whenever Coyote is killed, he can make himself come to life again, but it took him the whole night to puff himself up into his usual shape. In the morning the rancher's wife told her husband, "I just saw your rug running away."

Friends, hear this: always be generous in heart. If you have something to give, give it forever.

—Told by Jenny Leading Cloud in White River, Rosebud Indian Reservation, South Dakota, 1967. Recorded by Richard Erdoes.

INTRODUCING THE STORY

Although this story can be appreciated without explanation, it becomes more meaningful in light of the American Indian tradition of giveaway. We explain to the children that in many tribes, a person is considered wealthy and powerful not because of the many valuable things he *owns,* but because of the many valuable things he *gives away.* A person who is not generous is not admired, and to take back what one has given, as Coyote does, is unthinkable. The tradition of giveaway continues today at Indian pow-wows and potlatches.

The *wasichu* rancher is a white man; *wojapi* is berry soup.

The storyteller's statement that Iya, the rock, was covered with lines of moss that "tell a story" brings to mind the Native American tales of storytelling rocks. In these tales, a rock is the source of the legends or stories of a tribe. See the title story in Dorothy DeWit's *The Talking Stone,* and "The Coming of Legends" in *Iroquois Stories* by Joseph Bruchac.

TIPS FOR STORYTELLING

Much of "Coyote, Iktome, and the Rock" is told in the form of dialogue between the characters. Since the children listening need to draw inferences about the characters' motivations from what they are saying, it is usually helpful if the storyteller pauses often. Children love the idea of a wise, talking rock. They eagerly await Coyote's punishment. They are not surprised when Coyote resuscitates himself—that is what he always does in cartoons.

The text of this story includes a moral, directed to the audience by the storyteller, Jenny Leading Cloud, from whom it was recorded. You will probably want to restate this in your own words, or let the audience decide what lessons can be learned from this tale.

Participation Storytelling

The audience can participate in Coyote and Iktome's flight from the rolling rock. The storyteller divides the audience into two parts. One part practices making the deep "rumble, rumble, rumble" of Iya, the rock. The other

half makes the desperate cries of Coyote and Iktome. The
storyteller can then use the audience for sound effects, cueing
them like an orchestra conductor. Be sure to practice your
cues for starting and stopping the sounds until the children
can do both perfectly.

CREATIVE DRAMATICS

Coyote Rugs

The children lie on the floor and make themselves
as flat as they possibly can as the leader narrates:

> You are Coyote, lying on the floor of the ranch-
> er's living room. Iya, the rock, rolled over you
> and now you are as thin as a sheet of paper. You
> are barely breathing. It is nighttime. Everyone is
> asleep. The house is quiet. You gather up all
> your power, and slowly, you begin to puff up
> your hind leg . . .

The leader continues to narrate, slowly, to the
beat of the drum, as the coyotes puff up first one part of their
bodies, then another. Coyotes can then get up and walk
around. Perhaps they puffed up a bit too much, and need to
deflate.

Somersault Transformations

Iktome changed into a spider by doing a somersault. The children can do the same, first deciding what

animal they will become, then somersaulting and freezing in position as that animal. It is difficult, if not impossible, to have a large group doing somersaults at the same time. Divide the group into sections of four or five children, then have one section at a time perform the activity. "Somersault transformations" can also be used as a game in which the other children guess what animal the child has become.

Scene Play

The entire story may be acted out in the creative dramatics circle; the leader narrates transitions, and the children improvise action and dialogue. Drama takes place in the middle of the circle, and the leader changes the cast at the beginning of each new scene. A group of three or four children can play Iya, the rock, perhaps speaking together in an eerie voice (they will have to plan and rehearse Iya's lines in order to do this). Chasing and running should be done "in place."

CREATIVE WRITING

Comic Strip

Scenes from "Coyote, Iktome, and the Rock" can be drawn as a sequence of three cartoon frames, with the characters' words and thoughts written in balloons above their heads. Brainstorm first with the group to identify two or three of the best (most visual) scenes for cartooning, and divide each scene into a sequence of three cartoon frames, writing brief descriptions of these frames on the board. Most children want to portray the angry rock coming after Coyote; the sequence of three frames for this scene could be (1) Coyote taking back the blanket, (2) Iya chasing Coyote and Iktome, and (3) Iya squashing Coyote as Iktome rolls into a mousehole. The ideas you brainstorm will be a helpful starting point for some children; others may want to use their own ideas for content and format.

Letter-writing

In this activity, each child writes a letter from one of the story characters to a friend, describing Coyote's encounter with Iya, the Rock. The leader writes the name of each character on the chalkboard, and the group discusses the reactions—particularly feelings—of each one to the events of the story. Writers can take the point of view of Iya, Iktome, Coyote, or the rancher. The leader should encourage the writers to add what they imagine the characters may have thought or felt about what happened, as well as any added details that their character remembers about the events in the tale.

The Nungwama

CHINA

There was once an old woman who lived with her little granddaughter. One day the old woman was out gathering firewood, when she saw a green stalk of sugarcane lying on the ground. The old woman added the sugarcane to her bundle of sticks.

Suddenly she heard a grunting and a growling, and from behind a tree, there appeared the Nungwama. The hideous Nungwama was covered all over with dirty, shaggy fur, and its great foaming mouth was full of long, pointed, orange teeth.

"That is *my* sugarcane," roared the Nungwama. "Give it to me."

"No," replied the woman. "I found it, and I am taking it home to my little granddaughter."

"In that case," the Nungwama chortled, "tonight I shall come to your house and eat your little granddaughter." And he disappeared, laughing, into the woods.

The old woman went home, and sat on her doorstep, and began to cry, for she had no way to protect her granddaughter from the horrible Nungwama.

Now, there was a road that ran past the old woman's house, and down that road came a man pushing a wheelbarrow full of cow manure. He asked the old woman why she was crying.

"The Nungwama says he is coming here tonight to eat my little granddaughter," she said.

"When the Nungwama says he is coming, that means he will certainly come," said the manure-seller sadly. "Here is some cow manure. Spread it on your front door tonight. Perhaps the Nungwama will get his hands dirty, and go away, and leave you alone."

The old woman thanked the man, and took the cow manure, and spread it on the front door. Then she sat down on her doorstep, and continued to cry.

Along came a young man carrying a pole across his shoulders. From each end of the pole there hung a bucket of water filled with fish. The young man asked the old woman why she was crying.

"The terrible Nungwama says he is coming tonight to eat my little granddaughter," she said.

"The Nungwama always keeps his promise," said the fish-seller. "Take these two poisonous fish, and put them in a bucket of water near your bed. Perhaps the Nungwama will want to wash his hands in the water, and the poisonous fish will bite him, and he will run away."

The old woman thanked the man, and she put the two poisonous fish into a bucket of water by her bed. Then she sat on the doorstep and resumed her crying.

Along came a girl carrying a basket full of eggs on her head. She asked the old woman why she was crying.

"Tonight, the Nungwama is coming to my house to eat my little granddaughter," she said.

"To be eaten by the Nungwama is not a pleasant

way to die," said the egg-seller. "Take two of my eggs, and put them in the ashes of your fireplace. Perhaps the Nungwama will come close to the fire and touch the eggs. Then the eggs will explode and blow ashes into his eyes, and he will run away."

The woman thanked the egg-seller, and she went to put the two eggs in the ashes of the fire. Then she sat on her doorstep and began to cry.

Down the road came a young boy carrying a snapping turtle. He asked the old woman why she was crying.

"The Nungwama is coming here tonight, and he is going to eat up my little granddaughter," she said.

"Take this snapping turtle," said the boy, "and put it under your granddaughter's bed. Perhaps the Nungwama will slide his long, floppy toes under the bed, and the turtle will bite him, and he will run away."

The old woman thanked the boy, and she put the snapping turtle under her granddaughter's bed. Then she sat down on her doorstep and began to cry.

Two men came along the road carrying shovels on their shoulders. They stopped to ask the old woman why she was crying.

"Tonight, the horrible Nungwama is coming to eat my little granddaughter," she said.

"We will dig a deep hole behind your house. Perhaps the Nungwama will come to your house after dark, and will not see the hole, and will fall into it," said the man, and they set to work and dug a deep pit by the old woman's house. She thanked them kindly, then sat down on her doorstep and continued to cry.

Four men appeared then, rolling a huge millstone down the road. When they saw the old woman, they stopped to ask her why she was crying.

"The terrible Nungwama is coming here tonight to eat my granddaughter," she said.

"The Nungwama has been terrorizing the whole country," the men said. "We will take this millstone, and prop it up on the edge of that pit by your house. If the Nungwama falls into the pit, the millstone will fall in after him and crush him."

The old woman thanked the men. Then, as it was getting dark, she went inside her house and she and her granddaughter got into bed. Fearfully they waited for the footsteps of the terrible Nungwama. There they were: flum, flum, flum, flum, flum, flum. The Nungwama pushed against the front door.

"Ooooh! Phewwww!" he yelled. "Cow manure! There is cow manure all over my hands." He rushed into the house, and shoved his hands into the pail of water that sat by the door.

"OWWWWW! Something has bitten me! Something has bitten me!" The Nungwama ran toward the fireplace. He meant to put ashes on his hands where the poisonous fish had bitten him. He reached into the embers and POP! POP! the two eggs exploded, sending hot cinders into his eyes.

"Help! I can't see." He groped and tripped and stumbled until he came to the bed of the little granddaughter. "Crrrrunch." The snapping turtle bit his floppy big toe.

"Ow! Ow! Ow! Ow! Ow!" he cried, as he hopped out the door and into the yard and . . .

The Nungwama disappeared into the pit, and the millstone fell in after him, and that was the end of him. There was a large reward for the person who captured that miserable monster, and the old woman gladly shared it with all the people who had helped her.

INTRODUCING THE STORY

The Nungwama is a mysterious forest-dwelling monster. In other versions of the tale, the creature is a tiger or a wild boar. Though he is very frightening at the beginning, by the end of the story, the Nungwama has turned into a big, laughable sissy. We like to introduce the story with contemporary monster riddles which play on the serious/silly ambivalence of our own attitudes toward monsters, such as:

> What do you say to a two-headed monster?
> "How do you do, sir? How do you do, sir?"

> What do you do with a blue monster?
> Cheer him up.

> Where does a two-thousand-pound green monster sleep?
> Anywhere he wants to.

TIPS FOR STORYTELLING

This is not a story that needs to be told word for word, but the storyteller must prepare the trap for the Nungwama carefully, making sure to have the monster encounter each part of the trap in order when he arrives at the old woman's house.

After each person describes his gift to the old woman, pause so that the children have time to guess how that particular object will be used against the Nungwama. The pace of the story quickens after the arrival of the Nungwama at the woman's house. Younger children especially enjoy hearing the storyteller act out the beast's anguished cries.

CREATIVE DRAMATICS

Warm-ups

The group retells the story, recalling the order in which the various people walked by the old woman's house and discussing how each one was carrying the various objects and creatures they gave her. The leader begins narrating a random walk in which the children imagine they are first one character, then another: the woman gathering firewood, the Nungwama, the man pushing a wheelbarrow (don't run into anyone else's wheelbarrow!), the person carrying two pails of poisonous fish on the ends of a pole (stay away from the buckets!), the girl with a basket of eggs on her head, the boy carrying the snapping turtle, and the pair carrying shovels. They will have to work in groups to roll the heavy millstone. Each of these activities is unusual and should elicit a high degree of concentration from the children. As narrator, the leader emphasizes dangerous situations with warnings like "Hold your snapping turtle by the sides of its shell, with the head pointed away from you. Don't come too close to anyone else's snapping turtle" and "Keep the millstone upright; don't let it fall over on its side. Keep it rolling, but don't let it roll away from you."

Building a House

This pantomime activity requires intense concentration. The children are divided into work crews that will build the old woman's house. It is a simple house, with only one room. The entire group will first discuss the design of the house: how many doors, windows, beds, etc. Don't forget the fireplace, which plays an important part in the story. What are the walls made of? The roof? Each group is then assigned a job. One group lays the foundation, another group builds the walls, another the fireplace, then another group puts on the roof, and another furnishes the house. Each group must respect the imaginary constructions of the previous groups. No one may, for example, walk through a wall.

Scene Play

The opening scene of the story may be played simultaneously by pairs of children. The leader narrates as the old woman gathers wood, adds it to her bundle of sticks, and finds the sugarcane. With the arrival of the Nungwama, the children take over with their own improvised dialogue for the encounter between the old woman and the monster.

The imaginary house (above) may be used in the playing of the rest of the story. As the old woman sits crying on her doorstep, peddlers come by and offer to help her. In order to involve a large group, there may be multiple manure-sellers, boys with snapping turtles, etc. The group can sit in a semicircle, with children becoming characters in the story at the appropriate times. Before playing the final scene, where the Nungwama enters the house, the group can invent a sound effect for each object or creature the Nungwama will encounter, for example, "crunch, crunch!" for the snapping turtle. These can be either words or sounds. The leader narrates the final scene as a child playing the Nungwama enters the house, cueing the sound effects through pauses.

CREATIVE WRITING

Tombstone for the Nungwama

Suppose the Nungwama had been buried next to the old woman's house. What would be carved on the tombstone? The leader can help the group brainstorm the kinds of information that is found on tombstones, such as dates of birth and death, a short statement telling a bit about the person, even a poem or epitaph. They may wish to complete this couplet for the tombstone.

Here lies the body of the old Nungwama,

_____ .

Children we have worked with have come up with a number of playful and imaginative words which rhyme with Nungwama, such as mama, comma, pajama, and La Bamba! Mock tombstones may be made from white paper or white boxes.

Parallel Story

The basic plot of the Nungwama story is common throughout Asia. A Korean girl told us another version that she had heard from her mother: The old woman meets a tiger as she works in her garden. The tiger wants to eat her on the spot, but the woman persuades him to let her have a last meal so that she will be fatter. As she sits at her kitchen table, crying and eating kimchee, along come a banana peel, an egg, a straw mat, a nail, a rope, and a backpack. The woman shares her meal with each of them, and together they help her catch the tiger.

The children can create an ending to this story, in which these six objects await the tiger in certain parts of the house, and capture him.

In the version we heard, the banana peel lies on the floor, the egg in the fireplace, and the straw mat in front of the fireplace; the nail sticks in the ceiling; the rope lies by the mat; and the backpack waits in the yard. The tiger slips on the banana peel and skids in the fireplace, where the egg explodes in his face. He lands on the mat, which rolls him up, then the nail falls down and holds the mat while the rope ties it up. Finally the mat rolls the tiger onto the backpack, where he is ready for a strong person to carry him off to the king's palace. (Of course, the point of this writing activity is not to have the children come up with this exact scenario, but they will probably want to know "what really happened.")

Flea's-eye View

The leader begins this writing activity with guided imagery—this works best if the children close their eyes. The children imagine they are shrinking—getting smaller, smaller, smaller—until they are the size of a grain of sand.

> You are so small, it would take you an hour just to walk to the edge of your chair. But wait! You don't have to walk; you can jump. You can jump high, a hundred times as high as your body. Imagine in your mind's eye that you are a flea. Imagine that you take a big jump. And another. When you land, you don't feel a thing, because you have a hard, thick shell. You have landed in a thick forest. You can't see anything. Take another jump. Up. Higher. Higher. There. Oh, my. The forest is moving. It isn't a forest at all. It's thick fur. You are standing on the very top of the head . . . of the Nungwama. It's nighttime. Everything is dark. Wait . . . you see a light up ahead. It is coming from a small house, the house of the old woman. Pick up your pencil and start to write, "The Nungwama reaches for the old woman's front door. . . ."

The Pied Piper

A very long time ago, the town of Hamlin in Germany was invaded by armies of rats, the like of which had never been seen before nor will ever be seen again.

They were great, huge creatures that ran boldly in broad daylight through the streets, and swarmed all over the houses, so that people could not put a hand or foot down anywhere without touching one. When dressing in the morning, they found them in their breeches and petticoats, in their pockets and their boots. And when they wanted a bite to eat, the rats had gotten to it first.

Neither cats nor dogs, nor poison nor traps, nor prayers nor candles burnt to all the saints—nothing would help. The more they killed, the more came. The citizens of Hamlin were in great despair, when one Friday there arrived in the town a man with an odd face who played on the bagpipes and sang,

"Who lives shall see
That this is he,
The rat-catcher!"

He was a great gawky fellow, dry and bronzed, with a crooked nose, a long rat-tail moustache, two yellow piercing and mocking eyes, under a large felt hat set off by a scarlet feather. He was dressed in a green jacket with a leather belt and red breeches, and on his feet were sandals fastened by thongs passed round his legs in the gipsy fashion.

That is how he may be seen to this day, painted on a window of the cathedral in Hamlin.

He stopped at the marketplace before the town hall, turned his back on the church, and went on with his music singing,

> "Who lives shall see,
> That this is he,
> The rat-catcher!"

The town council had just assembled to consider once more this plague from which no one could save the town. The stranger sent word to the council that, if they would make it worth his while, he would rid them of all their rats before nightfall.

"Then he is a sorcerer!" cried the citizens. "We must beware of him."

The town counsellor reassured them. "Sorcerer or not, if this piper speaks the truth, it was he who sent us these horrible vermin in the first place. Well, we must learn to catch the devil in his own snares. Leave it to me."

"Leave it to the town counsellor," said the citizens to one another. And the stranger was brought before them.

"Before night," said he, "I shall have dispatched all the rats in Hamlin, if you will but pay me a gros a head."

"A gros a head!" cried the citizens, "but that will come to millions of florins!"

The town counsellor simply shrugged his shoulders and said to the stranger, "A bargain! And to work; the rats will be paid one gros a head as you ask!"

The piper announced that he would begin that very evening when the moon rose. When the people of Hamlin heard of the bargain, they too exclaimed, "A gros a head? Surely this will cost us a great deal of money."

"Leave it to the town counsellor," said the town council with a malicious air. And the good people of Hamlin repeated, "Leave it to the town counsellor."

Towards nine that night, the piper reappeared on the marketplace. He turned his back to the church, and the moment the moon rose on the horizon, "Tra-ri-ra, tra-ri," the bagpipes resounded.

Soon, from the bottom of the cellars, the top of the garrets, from under all the furniture, from all the nooks and the corners of the houses, out came the rats, searching for the door, flinging themselves into the street, and trip, trip, trip, running in rows toward the front of the town hall, so squeezed together that they covered the pavement like a wide river of rats.

Still playing the same tune, the piper led the rats to the edge of the river that runs by the foot of the walls of Hamlin. "Hop! hop!" he cried, pointing with his finger to the middle of the stream, where the water whirled and was drawn down as if through a funnel. And hop! hop! without hesitating, the rats took the leap, swam straight to the funnel, plunged in head foremost and disappeared.

The plunging continued thus without ceasing till midnight. At last, dragging himself with difficulty, came a big rat, white with age. It was the king of the rats.

"Are they all there, friend Whitewhiskers?" asked the piper.

"They are all there," replied Whitewhiskers.

"And how many were they?"

"Nine hundred and ninety nine thousand, nine hundred and ninety-nine."

"Then go and join them, old sire, and farewell."

Then the old white rat sprang in his turn into the river, swam into the whirlpool, and disappeared.

When the piper had finished his business, he went to bed at the inn. And for the first time in three months, the people of Hamlin slept quietly through the night.

The next morning, at nine o'clock, the bagpiper went to the town hall, where the town council awaited him.

"All your rats took a jump into the river yesterday," said he to the counsellors, "and I guarantee that not one of them comes back. There was exactly one million, at one gros a head. Count the money!"

"Let us count the *heads* first. One gros a head is one head the gros. Where are the heads?"

The rat-catcher paled with anger and his eyes flashed fire. "The heads!" cried he, "If you care about them, go and find them in the river."

"So," replied the town counsellor, "you refuse to hold to the terms of your agreement? We ourselves could refuse you all payment. But you have been of use to us, and we will not let you go without recompense. We will pay you fifty crowns."

"Keep your money for yourself," replied the rat-catcher. "If you do not pay me all that you owe me, then I will be paid by your children." He pulled his hat down over his eyes and left the town without speaking to anyone.

When the people of Hamlin heard how the affair had ended, they laughed at the rat-catcher who, they said, was caught in his own trap. But what made them laugh above all was his threat of getting himself paid by their children. Ha! They wished that they would have such creditors for the rest of their lives.

The next day, which was Sunday, they all went happily to church, thinking that after mass they would at last be able to eat some good thing that the rats had not tasted before them. They never suspected the terrible surprise that awaited them on their return home. No children anywhere! They had all disappeared.

"Our children! Where are our children?" was the cry that soon echoed through all the streets. Then through the east door of the town came three little boys, crying and weeping, and this is the story they told:

While the parents were at church, a wonderful music had resounded. Soon all the little boys and little girls who had been left at home had gone out and followed the magical sounds to the marketplace. There stood the rat-catcher, playing his bagpipes—Tra-ri-ra, tra-ri—at the same spot as the evening before. Then the stranger had begun to walk quickly, and they had followed, running, singing, and dancing to the sound of the music, as far as the foot of the mountain that one sees on entering Hamlin. At their approach the mountain had opened a little, and the bagpiper had gone in with them, after which it had closed again. Only the three little ones who told of the adventure had remained outside. One could not run fast enough, another had hurt his foot, and the third had bumped against the mountain in his haste and fell backwards at the moment the door closed.

When they heard this, the parents took pikes and

hammers and shovels and raced to the mountain, hoping to find the opening through which their children had disappeared. But at last, night falling, they returned desolate to Hamlin. Most unhappy of all was the town counsellor, for he had lost three little boys and two little girls, and the people of Hamlin overwhelmed him with reproaches, forgetting that the evening before they had all agreed with him.

What had become of all these unfortunate children? The parents always hoped they were not dead, and that the rat-catcher would have taken them with him to his country. That is why, for several years, they sent in search of them to different countries, but no one ever came on a trace of the little ones.

It was not until much later that anything was to be heard of them. About one hundred and fifty years after, when there was no longer anyone left of the fathers, mothers, brothers, or sisters of that day, there arrived one evening in Hamlin some merchants of Bremen returning from the east, who asked to speak with the citizens. They told that they had traveled to Hungary, and had come across a mountainous country called Transylvania, where the people spoke only German, while all around them nothing was spoken but Hungarian. These people declared that they came from Germany, but they did not know how they chanced to be in this strange country.

"Now," said the merchants of Bremen, "these Germans cannot be other than the descendants of the lost children of Hamlin." The people of Hamlin did not doubt it, and certainly there are more difficult things to believe than that!

INTRODUCING THE STORY

Music can enliven the transition from desks to story-circle. Recorded bagpipe music would be used to introduce "The Pied Piper." Ask the children to listen to the music and to imagine what sort of role that music could play in a story.

The word "pied" means multicolored, and refers to the piper's motley clothing.

TIPS FOR STORYTELLING

"The Pied Piper" is retold in a literary form that needs to be learned and told nearly word for word. Most children *think* they know the story of the Pied Piper, but few really do. We like to begin the story without announcing the title, so that the realization dawns on the children slowly that they have heard of this tale before.

CREATIVE DRAMATICS

Rat Warm-ups

The leader narrates as the children become rats:

Feel your pointed nose and long whiskers. Comb your whiskers with your paws. Swish your tail around. Now, let's take a walk around the kitchen. Climb up on the table. Look around. Oh, there's some butter. Let's take a taste. Now

let's leave some paw prints in it. Shall we climb
up the curtains . . . ?

At the end of the activity, the little rats can gather
in small groups and plan the things they will do that day to
annoy the people of Hamlin.

Rat-catching Machine

The group should first have completed the machine activity in the Creative Dramatics chapter. The challenge of the rat-catching machine is to make a machine that
either lures the rats into its trap, or else (and this is much
more difficult) *moves* to catch the rats. Obviously, the
machine the children make with their bodies could never
really catch anyone. The children playing the role of the rats
must agree to be caught.

This activity can be played many times, with one
part of the group making the machine and the other part
playing the rats.

Scene Play: Complaining to the Town Council

Begin with all children playing the roles of the
citizens of Hamlin. The leader coaches them to lie down,
still, sleeping. Slowly, they awaken and dress, but in the
midst of dressing, they find a rat. Each child decides where
the rat is and grabs it. Together, holding up the rats by their
tails, the citizens march off to see the town council.

At this point, the leader assigns half the group to
play the role of the town council. Each angry citizen walks

up to a member of the town council, shows the rat, and complains about all the problems the rats are causing in the town. The counsellors try to calm the angry citizens. A third group could enter in at this point, playing the part of reporters interviewing the townspeople and the town counsellors about the great plague of rats.

CREATIVE WRITING

Advertisement

Suppose the rat-catcher advertised his services by leaving posters at everyone's door. What kind of a picture would be on the poster? What would he claim to do? Would he list his price on the poster? Would he tell how long he has been in business? Give quotes from satisfied customers in other towns.

Diary

What happened after the children in the story left with the Pied Piper? Ask your group to imagine that *they* are the children the rat-catcher led into the mountain. They are to write a diary entry telling of that first day when they followed the strange man out of town and through the door and into the mountain. Before writing, the group can brainstorm what the inside of the mountain might have looked like, what possible dangers the children may have confronted there, where they spent the first night, and how they finally came out of the mountain.

Wiley and the Hairy Man

UNITED STATES

Wiley's daddy was a bad man and a no-account. He went out thieving in the dark of the moon, slept while the weeds grew higher than the vegetables, and, what's worse, he robbed a corpse laid out for burying. So everybody thought that the Hairy Man would probably get him. That must have been what happened, because they never found him after he fell off the ferry boat. They looked for him a long way down the river, and in the still pools between the sandbanks, but they never found Wiley's daddy. Then they heard someone laughing from across the river, and everybody said, "That's the Hairy Man." So they stopped looking.

"Wiley," his mama told him, "the Hairy Man's got your daddy, and he's going to get you, too, if you don't look out."

"I'll look out," said Wiley. "I'll take my hound dogs everywhere I go. The Hairy Man can't stand hound dogs."

Wiley knew that because his mama had told him so. And she knew because she was from the swamps by the Tombigbee River, and she knew conjure magic.

One day, Wiley took his axe and went down in the swamp to cut some poles for a hen-roost, and his hound dogs went with him. But the dogs took out after a wild pig, and they ran so far off, Wiley couldn't even hear them yelp.

"I hope that old Hairy Man isn't anywhere around here now," Wiley thought.

He picked up his axe to start cutting poles, but he looked up and there came the Hairy Man through the trees grinning. He sure was ugly, and his grin didn't help much. He was hairy all over. His eyes burned like fire, and spit drooled over his big teeth.

"Don't look at me like that," said Wiley. Then Wiley noticed that the Hairy Man didn't have feet like a man. He had feet like a cow. Now, Wiley recollected he had never seen a cow up in a tree, so he threw down his axe and climbed lickety-split up a big bay tree.

"How come you climbin' trees?" the Hairy Man said.

"My mama told me to stay away from you. What you got in that big croaker-sack?"

"I ain't got nothin' . . . yet."

"Go on away from here," said Wiley, hoping the bay tree would grow some more.

"Ha," said the Hairy Man and picked up Wiley's axe. He swung it stout, and the chips flew. Wiley grabbed the tree close, rubbed his belly on it, and hollered,

"Fly, chips, fly,
Back in your same old place!"

The chips of wood flew right back into the trunk of the tree, and that Hairy Man cussed and cussed. He started in swinging the axe harder, and Wiley knew he'd have to holler fast.

"Fly, chips, fly,
Back in your same old place!"

They went to it tooth and nail then, Wiley hollering and the Hairy Man chopping. Wiley hollered till he was hoarse and he saw the Hairy Man gaining on him. Wiley had just about yelled himself out when he heard his hound dogs yelping way off. "Hey-yo, dogs!" he hollered.

"Fly, chips, fly,
Back in your same old place!
Fly, chips, fly,
Back in your same old place!"

"You ain't got no dogs," said the Hairy Man. "I sent that pig to draw 'em off."

"Hey-yo dogs," hollered Wiley, and they both heard the hound dogs yelping.

"Come on down," shouted the Hairy Man, "and I'll teach you conjure."

"I can learn all the conjure I want from my mama."

Those dogs came running straight to the bay tree. The Hairy Man cussed some more, but he threw the axe down and lit out through the swamp.

When Wiley got home he told his mama that the Hairy Man had almost got him.

"Did he have his sack?"

"Yes."

"Next time he comes after you, don't climb up a bay tree."

"I won't," said Wiley. "They aren't tall enough."

"Don't climb any kind of tree. Just stay on the ground and say, 'Hello, Hairy Man.' You hear me, Wiley?"

"No, ma'am."

"He won't hurt you, child. You can put that old Hairy Man in the dirt when I tell you how."

"I put him in the dirt, and he puts me in that croaker-sack. I don't want to put the Hairy Man in the dirt."

"You just do like I say. You say, 'Hello, Hairy Man.' He says, 'Hello, Wiley.' You say, 'Hairy Man, I heard you're about the best conjure man around here.' 'I reckon I am.' You say, 'I bet you can't turn yourself into a giraffe.' You keep telling him he can't, and he will. Then you say, 'I bet you can't turn yourself into an alligator.' And he will. Then you say, 'Anybody can turn themself into something big as a man, but I bet you can't turn yourself into a possum.' Then he will, and you grab him and throw him into his own sack."

So Wiley tied up his dogs so they wouldn't scare away the Hairy Man, and went down to the swamp again. He hadn't been there long when he looked up and there came the Hairy Man grinning through the trees, hairy all over and his big teeth showing bigger than ever. He knew Wiley came off without his hound dogs. Wiley wanted to climb a tree when he saw him, but he didn't.

"Hello, Hairy Man," said Wiley.

"Hello, Wiley." The Hairy Man took the sack off his shoulder and started opening it up.

"Hairy Man, I heard you're about the best conjure man around here."

"I reckon I is."

"I bet you can't turn yourself into a giraffe."

"That ain't no trouble at all," said the Hairy Man.

"I bet you can't do it."

So the Hairy Man twisted round and turned himself into a giraffe.

"I bet you can't turn yourself into an alligator," said Wiley.

The giraffe twisted around and turned into an alligator, all the time watching Wiley to see he didn't try to run away.

"Anybody can turn themselves into something big as a man," said Wiley, "but I bet you can't turn yourself into a possum."

The alligator twisted around and turned into a possum. Possum's the slowest animal there is. Wiley grabbed that possum and threw it into the sack.

Wiley tied the sack up as tight as he could and then he threw it in the river. He started home through the swamp and he looked up and there came the Hairy Man grinning through the trees. Wiley climbed up the nearest bay tree.

"How'd you get out of that sack, Hairy Man?"

"I turned into the wind, and blew myself out. Wiley, I'm going to set right here till you get hungry and fall out of that bay tree."

Wiley studied awhile. He studied about the Hairy Man and he studied about his hound dogs tied up a mile away.

"Well," Wiley said, "you did some pretty smart tricks. But I bet you can't make things disappear and go where nobody knows."

"That's what I'm real good at. See that old bird's nest on that limb. Now it's gone!"

"How do I know it was there in the first place? I bet you can't make something I know is there disappear."

"Ha, ha," said the Hairy Man. "Look at your shirt."

Wiley looked down and his shirt was gone, but he didn't care because that was just exactly what he wanted the Hairy Man to do.

"That was just a plain old ordinary shirt," he said. "But this rope I got tied round my britches has been conjured. I bet you can't make *it* disappear."

"I can make all the rope in this county disappear."

"Ha, ha, ha," said Wiley.

The Hairy Man looked mad and threw his chest way out. He opened his mouth wide and hollered loud.

"From now on all the rope in this county has done *disappeared!*"

Wiley reared back, holding his britches up with one hand and holding onto the tree limb with the other hand.

"Hey-yo, dogs!" he hollered loud enough to be heard more than a mile off.

When Wiley and his dogs got back home, his mama asked him if he put the Hairy Man in the sack.

"Yes, but he turned himself into the wind and blew right through that old croaker-sack."

"That *is* bad," said his mama. "But you fooled him twice. If you fool him again, he'll leave you alone. He'll be mighty hard to fool the third time."

Wiley's mama sat down by the fire and held her

chin between her hands and studied real hard. But Wiley
wasn't studying anything except how to keep the old Hairy
Man away. He took his hound dogs and sat one down on the
front porch and one on the back porch. Then he crossed a
broom and an axe-handle over the window and built up a
fire in the fireplace. Feeling a lot safer, he sat down and
helped his mama study. After a little while, his mama said,
"Wiley, you go down to the pen and get that little tiny baby
pig."

Wiley went down and snatched the baby pig
through the rails. He took the pig back to his mama, and she
put it in his bed and covered it up with the quilt.

"Now, Wiley," she said, "you get under the bed
and hide."

So he did. Before long they heard the wind
howling and the trees shaking, and then Wiley's dogs started
growling. He looked out through a knothole in the planks
and saw the dog at the front door looking down toward the
swamp, with his hair standing up and his lips drawn back in
a snarl. Then an animal as big as a mule, with horns on its
head, ran out of the swamp past the house, and the dog lit
out after it. Then an animal bigger than a great big dog with
a long nose and big teeth ran out of the swamp and growled
at the cabin. This time, the other dog took after it down
toward the swamp.

"Now the Hairy Man's coming here sure," said
Wiley, and he hid under the bed. Sure enough, he heard
something with feet like a cow scrambling around on the
roof. He knew it was the Hairy Man, because he heard him
cuss and swear when he touched the hot chimney. The Hairy
Man jumped off the roof when he found out there was a fire

in the fireplace and came up and knocked on the front door as big as you please.

"Mama, I done come after your baby!" he hollered.

"You can't have him," Wiley's mama hollered back.

"Give him to me or I'll bite you and poison you."

"I'll bite you right back," Wiley's mama sang out.

"Give him here or I'll set your house on fire with lightning."

"I've got plenty of sweet milk to put out the fire."

"Give him here or I'll dry up your well, make your cow go dry and send a million boll-weevils out of the ground to eat up your cotton."

"Hairy Man, you wouldn't do all that. That's mighty mean."

"I'm a mighty mean man. I ain't never seen a man as mean as I am."

"If I give you my baby, will you go on away from here and leave everything else alone?"

"I swear that's just what I'll do," said the Hairy Man, so Wiley's mama opened the door and let him in.

"He's over in that bed," she said.

The Hairy Man came in grinning. He walked over to the bed and snatched the covers back.

"Hey," he hollered, "there's nothing in this bed but a little baby pig!"

"I didn't say what *kind* of baby I was giving

you, and that baby pig did belong to me before I gave it to you."

The Hairy Man raged and yelled. He stomped all over the house gnashing his teeth. Then he grabbed up the pig and tore out through the swamp, knocking down trees right and left. The next morning, it looked like a cyclone had cut through the swamp, with trees torn loose at the roots and lying on the ground. When the Hairy Man was gone, Wiley came out from under the bed.

"Is he gone, Mama?"

"Yes, child. That old Hairy Man can't ever hurt you again. We fooled him three times."

INTRODUCING THE STORY

Wiley's mother is a conjure woman. She knows how to use herbs and roots and charms, and how to work magic spells. The story can be introduced with a discussion of the kinds of magic worked, for good and evil, in folktales, such as shape changing and making objects appear and disappear. "Cinderella," "Puss in Boots," and "The Three Wishes" can be used as examples.

TIPS FOR STORYTELLING

This is a powerful story, and it is important for the storyteller to be faithful to the language and not leave out any details. Most retellers of this story omit the recitation of the sins of Wiley's father. We feel this is an important part of the tale. Wiley is escaping not only from the Hairy Man, but from the legacy of his father.

A gravelly, gruff voice suits the Hairy Man, as does his bad grammar. After a slow, mysterious opening, the pace of the story should be lively and factual. Hand motions can cue the audience to join in on Wiley's chants, "hey-yo dogs!" (hands cupped to mouth) and "Fly, chips, fly!" (clench hands, then flick fingertips out toward audience).

CREATIVE DRAMATICS

Swamp Noises

The eerie *noises* of the swamp are as vivid in the mind's eye as the scenery. The group recalls the sound they imagined while listening to the story: the splash of the river, the slobbery growl of the Hairy Man, the howl of the wind, the yelps of Wiley's dogs, the Hairy Man chopping the tree, the cries of those strange beasts the Hairy Man sends, the squeals of the baby pig. Children take turns trying to imitate these sounds, then the group can retell certain scenes complete with sound effects.

Conjure Tricks

The children try standing, walking, speaking, and laughing as they imagine the Hairy Man would. The leader plays the role of Wiley, daring the Hairy Man to turn into first one animal, then another, making up more animals than are actually in the story. As the Hairy Man, the children spin around and turn into each animal. Can they turn into the wind?

Scene Play

Practically all the scenes with the Hairy Man are good to play, particularly the tree-chopping scene (with Wiley standing on a chair or table), and the shape-changing scene. Each of these scenes may be played several times, in the center of the circle, changing the cast each time. Often, groups we worked with would want to act out a scene that is only alluded to in the story, the one in which Wiley's father falls into the river, the Hairy Man carries him off, and the people all look for him up and down the river.

CREATIVE WRITING

Wanted Poster

Create a wanted poster for the Hairy Man. Draw a picture of him (you may want to provide a front and side view, as some of the posters in the post office do), and tell about any distinctive marks or scars he has. What is he wanted for? Where was he last seen? What kind of reward is being offered?

Parallel Story

Write your own story in which you, or someone else, fool the Hairy Man. You might want to use this story-starter:

Winnie was a young girl, about thirteen years old. One day, she was fishing down by the river with her three dogs. There was an old fallen tree in the river, and her dogs started running back and forth across it to the other side. Pretty soon, that tree trunk floated away on the river, leaving Winnie's dogs trapped on the other side. Then, Winnie heard a kind of laughing noise behind her. It sounded a lot like the Hairy Man. . . .

Suho

MONGOLIA

In Mongolia, the people play a musical instrument called the horse-head fiddle. It is about the size of a violin, and at the very top of the neck is a carving of a horse's head. If the horse-head fiddle could talk, this is the story it would tell.

Once a young shepherd named Suho lived on the steppe, the broad treeless grassland of Mongolia. Suho was an orphan and he had been raised by his grandmother. Together, they owned a flock of sheep, and it was Suho's job to take the sheep out to graze on the steppe each morning, and to bring them back each evening. Suho worked as hard as any man, although he was scarcely more than a boy. In the evenings, he and his friends would gather in one of the tents, and tell stories, and laugh, and sing. The finest of all the singers was Suho.

Early one morning, Suho left with his flock of sheep; but by nightfall, they had not yet returned home. His grandmother was worried. All the neighbors had gathered, and were deciding whether to go out and search for Suho. Just then, they heard the bleating of his sheep. Far away in the darkness they could just barely see Suho. He was carrying something white. As he drew closer, they saw that it was a newborn foal.

"I found it alone, out on the steppe," Suho said.

"I waited and waited to see if its mother would return for it. Then darkness came, and I was afraid to leave it, for fear that the wolves might attack."

Suho cared for the colt, and it grew to be healthy and strong. Everyone admired it, and Suho loved it dearly.

One night, Suho was awakened by the sound of his colt's frantic cries, and by the frightened baaing of the sheep. He rushed to the sheepfold, and there he found the young colt bravely attacking a huge wolf who was trying to carry off one of the lambs. Suho chased the wolf away, then he patted the tired, frightened colt. Afterwards, Suho and his colt became inseparable.

A year passed. The colt grew into a splendid horse. When Suho rode him, people said they went faster than the wind, and that the horse's white coat shone like silver in the sun.

One day, exciting news arrived at Suho's village. The Khan had announced a great horse race. The winner of the race would receive the hand of the Khan's daughter in marriage. Suho's friends persuaded him to go to the capital and enter.

Many fine young men and many swift horses raced that day, but it was Suho, riding the white horse, who won.

"Bring the rider of the white horse here," commanded the Khan. As Suho approached the Khan's tent, the Khan saw that he was only a poor and lowly shepherd. When the Khan spoke to Suho, he did not even mention his daughter, but merely said, "Here are three bars of silver. These are your prize. You may leave your horse with my guards."

"I came here to enter a race, and win the hand of

your daughter!" cried Suho. "I have not consented to sell my horse."

"Insolent peasant!" screamed the Khan. He ordered his guards to beat Suho. They seized the white horse and led it away to the royal stables. Suho's friends carried him home, and his grandmother cared for him until his wounds healed. But nothing could heal the pain of losing his beloved horse.

The Khan had a splendid saddle made for the white horse, and held a grand celebration. He planned to ride on the white horse and impress everyone. But instead, as he mounted the horse in front of all the guests, the animal reared up and turned around and about wildly, until the Khan fell down to the ground. The horse galloped away.

"Catch him!" the Khan ordered his guards. But the horse ran too swiftly for them. "Shoot him!" cried the Khan to his archers, and they let fly their arrows. Many arrows pierced the white horse's side, but still the horse galloped on.

Late that night, Suho and his grandmother were awakened by a familiar noise outside their tent. "It is our white horse," said Suho's grandmother.

Suho rushed outside. There stood the horse, a dozen arrows in his side. Suho embraced his horse. The horse lay down, and before sunrise, he was dead.

Suho grieved for his dear friend. For two nights, he could not sleep. Then on the third night, he closed his eyes and dreamed. In the dream, his white horse stood before him and spoke to him.

"Do not be sad, Suho. Only take my bones, and my sinews, and my skin, and make from them a fiddle and a bow. That way, I can be near you whenever you sing and play music."

When Suho awoke, he was happy again. He took the horse's bones and skin and sinews, and he fashioned a fiddle and a bow. At the top of the fiddle's neck, he carved the head of his white horse.

In the evenings, when work was done and the shepherds gathered together to tell stories and sing, Suho would play the horse-head fiddle. As he played, the music brought back memories of the joy of riding his horse across the steppe, and everyone could delight in the beautiful sounds of Suho's music.

INTRODUCING THE STORY

The story of Suho contains its own introduction, but the audience may need a clearer picture of the steppes of Mongolia and the life of a shepherd. The picture book *Suho and the White Horse*, adapted by Yuzo Otzuka and illustrated by Suekichi Akaba, contains beautiful illustrations that effectively portray the setting of the story.

TIPS FOR STORYTELLING

The death of Suho's horse is quite sad, yet the theme of the story is the dignity of the individual and the healing power of artistic creation. The pathos of the tale should emerge in the words, not in any sad voice quality of the storyteller. It is particularly important to give the happy and exciting parts their due, and not to anticipate the later tragedy.

CREATIVE DRAMATICS

Warm-ups

While sitting in a circle, the children imagine they are out on the steppe, watching their sheep. As the leader narrates, they hear something, get up and walk toward the noise, and see that it is a baby horse. Gently they pick it up (one child had quite a struggle as the foal repeatedly jumped out of his arms) and carry it back to the circle.

Some of the children may know how to care for a horse. They can tell how to do this, then everyone can mime caring for an imaginary horse: first a newborn horse that needs to be bottle-fed, then an older horse that needs buckets of water to drink, and grass to eat, and daily brushing.

Scene Play

The group discusses Suho's dream—how Suho felt before he fell asleep, what the horse spirit said to him, and what Suho did after he awoke. What are the steps in making a horse-head fiddle? In pairs, children play the sleeping Suho and the horse spirit that appears in his dream.

Afterwards, all the children mime making and playing a horse-head fiddle.

CREATIVE WRITING

Song

Children familiar with writing poetry, rhymed or unrhymed, can write the words for a song, "My White Horse," to be played on the horse-head fiddle. If the group has not written poetry, the song can be a group creation, with the leader writing the words on a chalkboard or paper easel. The group can alternate sharing short statements about the horse with the line, "My white horse." This sort of activity is cathartic for a child who has heard the story, in the same way that the making of the instrument was for Suho.

Retelling the Story

The children take turns recalling and retelling their favorite part of the story. The leader makes a list of these episodes on the board, and also writes any difficult or unusual words. Then each child chooses an episode of the story to write, either as if he were Suho, or another character, such as one of Suho's friends.

Why the Sea Is Salt

NORWAY

Once upon a time, a long, long time ago, there were two brothers, one as rich as the other was poor. Now, one Christmas Eve, the poor brother hadn't so much as a crumb of bread or a scrap of meat in his house, so he went to ask his brother for something to feed his family, in God's name. It was not the first time the rich brother had been asked to help, so he was not happy to see the poor brother's face.

"Promise you will do exactly what I ask of you," said the rich man, "and you shall have a whole ham."

The poor man promised to do anything he said.

"Take this ham, and go straight and directly to the Devil!" The rich man shoved the ham into his hands, then he slammed the door in his brother's face.

So the poor man set off at once to find where the Devil lived. He walked and walked, and as darkness fell he came to a great house with bright lights shining in all the windows. And in a small woodshed by the gate stood an old man with a long white beard, chopping firewood.

"Good evening, grandfather."

"The same to you," answered the old man. "Where are you going with that ham?"

"I'm going to the Devil."

"And you've come to the right place," said the

old man, "for this is the house of the Devil himself. Now, when you go inside, everyone will want to buy your ham, for they never get any meat here. But do not let them have it unless they give you the hand-mill that stands behind the door. For that mill is magic, and when you get it from them, I'll teach you how to use it."

So the man went and gave a great knock at the Devil's door. When he got inside, all the great and small devils swarmed around him like ants and every one of them wanted to buy his ham.

"Well," said the man, "this was to be Christmas dinner for my family. But since you have all set your hearts on it, I suppose I must let you have it. But I will only trade it for the hand-mill that sits behind the door."

At first, the Devil wouldn't give up the mill. But then, at last, he wanted the ham so much, he had to part with it. At least, he thought, the man would never learn how to use it.

When the man got out into the yard, he asked the old woodcutter to show him the mill's magic. The old man said the mill would grind out anything the man wanted, if only he would say,

"Grind, mill, grind,
Grind fast and well,"

and then ask for whatever it was he wanted. Then the old man whispered in his ear the magic words to make the mill stop grinding. The man took the mill under his arm and he was home before the clock struck twelve on Christmas Eve.

He found his wife and children cold and hungry, with nothing to eat and not so much as two sticks to make a fire. He laid the mill on the table and commanded it to grind out first some firewood, then a tablecloth, then candles, then meat and ale, and everything they needed for a joyous Christmas feast. He had only to speak the words,

"Grind, mill, grind,
Grind fast and well,"

and the mill poured forth whatever he desired. He ground out food and drink and sweets to last through the holidays, and he invited all his friends and kin to a great feast.

When his rich brother saw what was on the table at the feast, he grew angry that his brother should have come into such good fortune.

"Only a few nights ago," he said to the other guests, "my brother was so destitute he had to come begging for a morsel of food. Now he gives a feast as if he were a count or a king."

Everyone demanded to know where he had gotten his wealth so suddenly. And, as the man had had a drop too much to drink, he brought out the mill and told them all how it would grind out whatever it was told. The rich brother set his heart on having the mill, and offered a fine price, and gave his brother no peace, so at last the man agreed to let him have the mill at hay-harvest time. For, he said to himself, by that time I shall have made it grind out enough to last me for years. And you may believe that the mill gathered no rust during that time.

When hay-harvest was over, the rich brother came to claim the mill, and the other brother showed him how to use it, saying,

"Grind, mill, grind,
Grind fast and well . . ."

but he took care *not* to teach him how to make it stop.

It was evening when the rich brother got the mill home. Next morning, when his wife had left to go to the fields, he took out the mill, placed it on the kitchen table, and said,

> "Grind, mill, grind,
> Grind fast and well,
> Grind out herrings and broth."

So the mill began to grind herrings and broth, and broth and herrings. First the dishes were full, then the tubs were full, then broth and herrings spilled onto the kitchen floor. And the man shouted for the mill to stop, but it kept on grinding until the man was likely to drown in herrings and broth. He grabbed the mill and flung open the kitchen door and ran into the parlor, but it wasn't long before the parlor, too, was full of herrings and broth, and the man lifted the latch of the front door and set off and ran down the road with the herrings swimming after him through the great river of broth that was lapping at his heels.

The man ran and ran to his brother's door, and he begged him to stop the mill before the whole county was covered in a great flood of herrings and broth. But the man wouldn't hear of it until the rich brother paid him another huge sum of money.

And so it was that the poor brother got both the money and the mill, and it wasn't long before he built a great fine house for himself, a house made entirely of gold. And, as the house perched upon a cliff overlooking the ocean, all who sailed by could see the gold house glistening and gleaming in the sun. One day a ship's captain stopped to visit the man, and when he heard about the wondrous mill, he asked could it grind salt.

"Grind salt!" said the owner. "I should think it could. It can grind anything."

Then the ship's captain said he must have the mill, no matter what the cost, for then he would no longer have to sail for years all over the world to bring back loads of salt. He could make the salt himself. At first the man wouldn't hear of selling the mill, but the captain begged and pleaded, and at last he let him have it at an enormous price.

When the captain had got the mill, he rushed off right away. He was afraid the man might change his mind about selling it, so he didn't even wait long enough to ask how to make it stop. He got on board his ship as fast as he could and set sail. When he had sailed a good way off, he brought the mill on deck and said,

"Grind, mill, grind,
Grind fast and well,
Grind out *salt!*"

And grind it did. Salt poured from the mill like water. And when the ship was full, the captain wanted to stop it, but whatever way he turned or twisted the mill, it was no use. The mill kept on grinding. The heap of salt grew higher and higher. The ship began to sink lower and lower into the water. At last, to save the ship and all on board from sinking, the captain had to toss the mill overboard.

Now the mill lies at the bottom of the sea and grinds away to this very day. And that is why the sea is salt.

INTRODUCING THE STORY

A story that took place before the sea was salt must be old indeed! To lead the audience gently into the fantastic events described in "Why the Sea Is Salt," we like to read them Lewis Carroll's "The Walrus and the Carpenter," a poem which is also both salty and fantastic.

We find it simplest to define the words "hand-mill," "herrings," and "broth" while telling the story. When each is first mentioned, we tell what it means in an aside to the audience, for example, "that's a little box with a crank on the side. You put grains of wheat in at the top, then turn the crank, and out comes flour."

TIPS FOR STORYTELLING

This story may be embellished with details the storyteller thinks the audience will appreciate—keeping in mind, of course, the time and place of the events' unfolding. For example, the storyteller may want to emphasize with details the contrast between the life of the poor brother and that of the rich brother, to describe the interior of the Devil's house, to tell other things that the poor man makes with the mill, or to invent a series of catastrophes caused by the flood of herrings and broth.

CREATIVE DRAMATICS

Magic Mill

The group decides on the imaginary layout of the poor brother's house. One child plays the poor man, and a group of five to ten children makes a mill-machine (see "Machine" in the Creative Dramatics chapter), complete with a handle that can be turned, and with an opening space through which a child can walk. The poor brother has decided to furnish his house luxuriously, now that he owns the mill. As he calls out each item that he wants (table, chair, rug, etc.), one of the remaining children passes through the magic mill, goes to the proper place in the house, and becomes that item.

Yes/No

"Yes/no" is a theater game in which students express intention and emotion using only the words "yes" and "no." The leader divides the group into pairs, with one member of each pair playing the role of the rich brother, the other the role of the poor brother. The leader then sets the scene; for example, the rich brother wants the mill ("yes") but the poor brother doesn't want to let him have it ("no"). The scenes are to last one minute, with the leader keeping time. At the end of the minute, the poor brother will have been convinced, but not without some hard work on the part of the rich brother, always using only one word: yes. Try the exercise again, using the scene in which the rich brother wants the poor brother to make the mill stop. The playing of the two scenes should be very different because of the different motivation. The leader may need to demonstrate the yes/no game to the entire group, but once they get the idea, they will have lots of fun with it.

Scene Play

The leader supplies drumbeats for dancing to begin the scene at the Devil's house. Negotiations for the mill between the poor man and the Devil can be modeled on the "yes/no" exercise above.

The leader can narrate, and the children mime, the scene of the captain bringing the mill on board his boat and commanding it to grind out salt. The leader beats the drum very slowly as the captain shows the mill to the crew and gives it the command to grind out salt. On each drumbeat, the crew and captain become happier and happier as they see how well the mill works; then gradually they become aware that the boat is sinking lower and lower with each drumbeat. The crew gesture to the captain to throw the mill overboard, and finally he does.

CREATIVE WRITING

Magic Words

What were the magic words to make the mill stop? You notice we left them out of the story. The children can write short poems to turn it off.

Outrageous Explanations

According to the story, the sea became salt because the brother gave the mill to a sea captain at the end of the story. Write a new ending to the story, in which the man gives the mill to someone else, and the mill is the cause of the sky being blue, the wind blowing, winter being cold, or the sun being hot.

The Liars' Contest*

GHANA

One day the fly, the moth, and the mosquito
went hunting together. They came upon Anansi in the
forest. "There is meat," they said, and they seized Anansi,
and there was a struggle. But Anansi was stronger than he
looked, and they were unable to overcome him. At last they
stopped to rest.

Anansi asked, "Why are you hunting me?"

They replied, "We are hungry. As you know, all
living things must eat."

Anansi said, "I also must eat. Why shouldn't I eat
you?"

"You aren't strong enough to subdue us," they
said.

"Nor are you strong enough to subdue me,"
Anansi said. "Let us make a bargain. You may tell me a
fantastic story. If I say I don't believe it, you may eat me. I
will tell you a story. If you say it isn't true, I will eat you."

The three hunters agreed. So the moth told his
story first.

"Before I was born," the moth said, "my father

---

* From *The Hat-Shaking Dance and Other Ashanti Tales from
Ghana* by Harold Courlander and Albert Kofi Prempeh.

settled on new land, but that very day he cut his foot with a bush knife and couldn't work. So I jumped up and cleared away the forest, cultivated the ground, planted it with corn, weeded it, harvested the corn, and put it in the granary. When I was finally born a few days later, my father was already a rich man."

The moth, the fly, and the mosquito looked at Anansi, waiting for him to say, "I do not believe it," so that they could eat him. But Anansi said: "How truly you have spoken! How true it is!"

Then the mosquito told his story. He said, "When I was only four years old, I was sitting peacefully in the forest chewing on an elephant that I had killed. But I felt like playing, and when I saw a leopard slink by, I chased him. When I was just about to catch him, he turned around and opened his jaws to swallow me. I quickly stuck my hand down his throat and seized the inside of his tail. Then I gave it a quick pull and turned the leopard inside out. The leopard had eaten a sheep. And now the sheep was on the outside and the leopard was inside. The sheep thanked me properly and grazed off into the grass."

The mosquito, the fly, and the moth waited for Anansi to say, "That is a lie," so they could begin eating him. But Anansi said, "Oh, how true! How true!"

So then the fly had his turn. He said, "This is my story. I went hunting in the forest one day and tracked down an antelope. I aimed my gun at him, fired, then ran forward and caught the antelope, turned him on his side, skinned him, and cut the meat into quarters. Just then the bullet which I had fired came along. I caught it and replaced it in my gun. I was hungry, so I carried the meat to the top of a tall tree, built a fire on a limb, and cooked a meal. I ate the entire antelope. When it was time to come down, I had eaten so much that my stomach was swollen, and I was too heavy to climb. So I went back to the village and got a rope. Then I returned to the tree, tied the rope around my waist, and let myself carefully down to the ground."

The fly, the moth, and the mosquito waited quietly for Anansi to say, "Oh, what an impossibility," but instead of that he said, "This is a true tale of true tales!"

Now it was Anansi's turn.

"Last year I planted a coconut tree," Anansi said. "One month later it was grown. I was hungry, so I cut three coconuts down. I opened the first nut with my bush knife, and a fly came out. I opened the second one, and a moth came out. I opened the third one, and a mosquito came out. As I had planted the tree on which they were grown, the fly and the moth and the mosquito belonged to me. But when I tried to eat them, they ran away. I have been searching for them ever since so that I could eat them. And now at last I have found you—my fly, my mosquito, and my moth."

The three hunters were silent.

Anansi asked, "Haven't you anything to say?"

They wanted to say, as Anansi had said, "How true, how true!" But they dared not, because then Anansi would claim them as his lost property and eat them. And they could not say he had lied, because then they would lose the contest, and Anansi would eat them. They couldn't make up their minds whether to cry truth or falsehood. At last they simply turned and fled.

And ever since then, whenever Anansi, the spider, catches flies, moths, or mosquitoes, he eats them, because he outwitted them in the lying contest.

INTRODUCING THE STORY

We usually begin this story by asking for a show of hands from the children who think that they might be able to win a liars' contest. Then we explain that the point of this particular liars' contest is not to tell a lie that people believe, but to tell a lie that is so fantastic, so unbelievable, so totally preposterous, that the person you are telling it to has no choice but to say "that's a lie!"

TIPS FOR STORYTELLING

"The Liars' Contest" is not an easy story to tell: there are many details which must be included in precise sequence. It is, however, a storyteller's delight, as older children follow it intensely, and are well rewarded when they "get" the point of Anansi's story. If you enjoy adding a bit of mime to your storytelling, this tale is ideal for it: moth, mosquito, fly, and Anansi would be very likely to act out their tall tales in order to make them appear even more fantastic.

Pause, and continue slowly, after Anansi announces *"my* moth, *my* fly, *my* mosquito." Watch the audience and make sure that most of them have gotten the point, before continuing to the end of the story.

CREATIVE DRAMATICS

Warm-up

Sitting in a circle, the children mime opening various things suggested by the leader, such as opening a peanut and eating it; opening your wallet and seeing a moth fly out; opening a can and having a spring snake shoot out; opening an envelope addressed to you and finding five hundred dollars. The children may want to add suggestions of their own for opening mimes.

Stage Fights

In groups of four—acting as the four characters in the story—children plan and rehearse a stage fight, one in which no one actually touches anyone else, yet it looks as if a fight is going on. To further assure that no one gets hurt, have them play it in slow motion. Limit the fights to one minute, let the groups rehearse several times, then let any groups that wish share their stage fight with the group.

Scene Play

In this activity, the children will all be playing the same characters at the same time; with no one watching, they are better able to concentrate. Children mime the lies of fly, moth, mosquito, and Anansi simultaneously as the leader retells the story. The leader should pause after each description of an action, in order to give the children time to pantomime it.

CREATIVE WRITING

Award Certificate

Design an award certificate to be given to the winner of the liars' contest. Be sure to include the date, place, and time of the contest, the name of the winner, and a description of the prize or prizes. Cut out or draw a blue and gold ribbon to go on the certificate.

Tall Tale

Usually, when a lie is told for fun, and not to trick or deceive anyone, it is called a tall tale. Write a tall tale about yourself and the incredible things you did when you were a baby. Begin the tall tale with the words, "When I was just one year old . . ."

The Three Golden Hairs of Grandfather Know-It-All

CZECHOSLOVAKIA

Once upon a time, there lived a king who was exceedingly fond of hunting the wild beasts of the forest. One day he followed a stag so far and so long that he lost his way. At last, the king came to the small, miserable cottage of a poor woodcutter and his wife, and he demanded lodging for the night.

The king lay down to rest on a mattress of fresh straw in the loft. Just after midnight, he was awakened by a strange, glowing light that filled the house. Looking down, he saw the woodcutter and his wife sleeping, and beside the woman lay a newborn baby. At the bedside stood three very old women, all dressed in white, each holding a burning candle in her hands. These, you must know, were the three Fates.

The first Fate said, "Upon this boy I bestow the gift of encountering great dangers."

The second Fate said, "I bestow upon him the power of overcoming all these dangers and living to a good old age."

The third Fate said, "I bestow upon him for his wife the princess born at the same hour as he, daughter of the very king sleeping upstairs in the loft."

At these words, the three women disappeared and all was silent.

Now, the king was greatly troubled, and he lay awake all night thinking how to prevent the words of the Fates from coming true. With the first glimmer of morning light, the baby began to cry. The woodcutter, going over to it, discovered that his wife was dead.

"Poor little orphan," he said sadly. "What will ever become of you?"

"Why not give the child to me?" said the king. "I will look after him, and he will be well taken care of."

The woodcutter gladly agreed, and the king went away promising to send someone for the child. When he arrived home, the queen thought it would be a great surprise for him to learn of the charming little princess that had been born in his absence. But instead of being pleased, the king frowned, and called in one of his servants. "Go to the woodcutter's cottage in the forest," the king commanded him, "and give the man this purse in exchange for his newborn son. On your way back, drown the child."

The servant was given the child in a basket, but he hadn't the heart to drown the boy. On reaching the banks of a river, he set both basket and baby in the stream and gave a push. The little one floated happily along until it floated past the cottage of a fisherman, who was sitting on the bank of the river mending his nets. The fisherman jumped into his boat and rowed after the babe and pulled him from the river.

The fisherman and his wife named the boy Plavachek, "the floatling," because he had come to them floating on the river. The river flowed on. Years passed away. Plavachek grew into a handsome youth. One summer day, the king was once again out hunting, and he reined in his horse at the fisherman's cottage to ask for a drink of water.

"Plavachek! Fetch a drink of water for the king," the fisherman called out to the young man.

"Plavachek? What an unusual name," said the king.

"I found him when he was a tiny babe, floating down the stream in a basket," said the fisherman. "We named him Plavachek, and have brought him up as our own son."

The king turned as pale as death, for he guessed that this was the same child he had ordered to be drowned. Then the king got down from his horse and said, "I need a messenger to take a letter to the queen. Could you spare Plavachek for the errand?"

The fisherman agreed, and the king wrote this letter to the queen,

> "The man who brings you this letter is a dangerous enemy. Have his head cut off at once."

Then the king carefully folded and sealed the letter with the royal seal.

Plavachek took the letter and set off immediately. But the forest through which he had to pass was so great, and the trees so thick, that he wandered off the path and was overtaken by darkness. At last, he saw a light coming from a small house in a clearing. Plavachek knocked at the door, and a woman let him in and showed him a bed, and he was soon asleep.

Now, this house belonged to a band of thieves and robbers, and when they got home that night, they searched Plavachek's pockets for anything valuable. They found the letter and opened it, and when they looked on the handsome youth, they thought it a shame that he should die. One of the robbers was also a master forger, and he wrote a new letter, copying the king's handwriting and cleverly transferring the king's seal to the new letter, which read:

> "Immediately upon receipt of this letter, introduce this young man to the princess, our daughter. I have chosen him to be my son-in-law, and it is my wish they should be married before my return."

The letter was delivered, and when the queen had read it, she ordered everything prepared for the wedding. Both she and the princess were very pleased with Plavachek, who was as kind as he was handsome.

When the king returned to the palace, he was furious. He could not undo what was done, but he set about to devise a plan to get rid of Plavachek once and for all. He called the young man to his chambers. "You will not become my son-in-law so easily, Plavachek, for you must first bring me a wedding gift in exchange for my daughter's hand. You will bring me three golden hairs from the head of Grandfather Know-It-All, who lives at the end of the world."

Plavachek set out, and he walked on and on for a long time, over mountain, valley and river, until he reached the shore of the Black Sea. There he found a boat and a boatman.

"May God bless you, old boatman," said he.

"And you, too, my young traveler. Where are you going?"

"To the castle of Grandfather Know-It-All for three of his golden hairs."

"For a long weary while I have waited for a messenger such as you," said the boatman. "I have been ferrying passengers across the Black Sea for twenty years. I will take you across, too, if you promise to ask Grandfather Know-It-All how I can be released from my labors."

Plavachek promised, and was rowed to the other side. He continued his journey until he came to a town. There he met an old, old man with a long white beard, sitting under a withered tree.

"God be with you, old man," said Plavachek.

"Thank you, good traveler. Where are you going?"

"To the castle of Grandfather Know-It-All," answered Plavachek.

"Ah, we have long been expecting a messenger such as you," cried the old man. "This apple tree once bore the fruit of everlasting youth. One of its apples eaten by a dying man would cure him and make him young again. But for the last twenty years, neither fruit nor flower has been found on the tree. Will you ask Grandfather Know-It-All the cause of this?"

"That I will, with pleasure," said Plavachek, and he set on his way again. He came to a large and beautiful city where all was sad and silent. Near the gate was an old man who leaned on a stick and walked with difficulty.

"May God bless you, old man," said Plavachek.

"And you, too, my handsome young traveler. Where are you going?"

"To the castle of Grandfather Know-It-All," replied Plavachek.

"Then you are the messenger we have long awaited," said the old man. "We have in this city a marvelous spring, and those who drink its water are immediately cured of any illness. A few drops of the water sprinkled on a corpse will bring it back to life. For the past twenty years, this well has remained dry. If you will ask old Grandfather Know-It-All how to restore the flow of water, I will reward you royally."

Plavachek promised to do so, and he traveled on through a dark forest, and in the center of the forest was a great meadow, carpeted with beautiful flowers, and in the center stood a castle all of gold, the castle of Grandfather Know-It-All. So brilliant with light was it that it seemed to be built of fire. When Plavachek entered, there was no one at home but an old woman, who sat spinning. When Plavachek told her his story, the woman said, "Grandfather Know-It-All is my son. He is a good boy, but when he gets home at night, he is very hungry, and would probably order you to be roasted for his supper. Here, I will turn you into an ant, and you can hide in the folds of my dress." So the woman turned Plavachek into an ant, and he hid beneath a fold in the cloth.

Suddenly a blast of wind howled round the palace, and the Sun entered by a western window. He was an old man with golden hair.

"I smell human flesh," cried he, "I am sure of it. Mother, do you have some one hidden here?"

"You, who know everything, would know

sooner than I," replied his mother. "You travel about the human world all day, and no doubt the scent has come home with you."

The old man ate supper, and when he had finished, he laid his golden head on the old woman's lap and went to sleep. Then, gently, she plucked out a hair from his head.

"What do you want, mother?" asked he.

"Oh, nothing my son. I was sleeping, and I had a strange dream. I thought I was in a city where there was a well, and the well was fed from a spring, the water of which cured all diseases. Even the dying were restored to health on drinking that water, and the dead who were sprinkled with it came to life again. For the last twenty years the well has run dry. What must be done to restore the flow of water?"

"That is very simple. A toad has lodged itself in the opening of the spring, and this prevents the flow of water. Kill the toad, and the water will return to the well."

He fell asleep again, and the old woman pulled out another golden hair, and threw it on the ground.

"Mother, what do you want?"

"Nothing, my son, I was only dreaming. In my dream, I saw a town, and in the town grew an apple tree, the fruit of which had the power to make the old young again. A single apple eaten by an old man would restore to him the strength of youth. For twenty years, this tree has not borne fruit."

"That is not a difficult problem," answered her son. "A rat is gnawing the roots of the tree. Kill the rat, and transplant the tree, and the fruit will grow as before."

He again fell asleep, and the old woman pulled out another golden hair.

"Now look here, Mother, why will you not let me sleep?" said the old man.

"I am sorry I awoke you, but I have had a very strange dream. It seemed that I saw a boatman on the shores of the Black Sea, and he complained that he had been toiling for twenty years without anyone having come to take his place. For how much longer must this poor man continue to row?"

"He is a silly fellow. He has but to place his oars in the hands of the first comer and jump ashore. Whoever receives the oars will replace him as ferryman. But leave me in peace now, Mother, and do not wake me again. I have to rise very early, and must first dry the eyes of a princess. The poor girl spends all night weeping for her husband, who has been sent by the king to get three of my golden hairs."

Next morning, the wind whistled round the castle, and instead of an old man, a beautiful child with golden hair awoke on the old woman's lap. It was the glorious sun. He bade her good-bye and flew out of the eastern window. The old woman turned Plavachek into a handsome youth again, and gave him the three golden hairs. He thanked her kindly, and left on his journey home.

When Plavachek arrived at the city of the water of life, he told the king, "Have the well cleaned out, and kill the toad who is blocking the spring, and your water will flow again."

The king did so, and rejoiced to see the water return. He gave Plavachek twelve swan white horses, and as much gold and silver as they could carry.

Plavachek reached the town of the apples of youth, and he told the king, "Dig up your apple tree, and kill the rat that lies among the roots. Transplant the tree, and it will produce apples as in former times."

All turned out exactly as he said, for no sooner was the tree replanted than it was covered with blossoms. The delighted king gave him twelve raven black horses laden with as much gold and silver as they could carry.

Then Plavachek journeyed to the shores of the Black Sea. The boatman questioned him as to what news he had brought. Plavachek first had the boatman row him and all his horses and treasures across. Then he told the man that he could gain his freedom by placing the oars in the hands of the very next traveller who wished to cross.

The king could not believe his eyes when he saw Plavachek, leading twelve black and twelve white horses, all laden down with treasure, and carrying the three golden hairs of Grandfather Know-It-All. He demanded to know how Plavachek had gotten the horses, gold, and silver.

"By showing one king how to regain possession of the apples of youth, and by showing another king how to reopen the spring of the water of life," said Plavachek.

"Apples of youth! Water of life!" shouted the king. "I will certainly go there and find these treasures for myself. I shall live forever!" The king set off in search of these treasures. Unfortunately, he has never been seen again. Perhaps it is because he went by way of the Black Sea.

INTRODUCING THE STORY

There are other "threes" in this story beside the three golden hairs of Grandfather Know-It-All. The number three is common in folktales and fairytales, both in titles (which often tell of the number of main characters), and in the number of episodes or adventures. Ask the children for examples of other stories in which "threes" play an important part; then have them to listen for things in this story which happens in threes.

TIPS FOR STORYTELLING

This is a long story, but, fortunately for the storyteller, it needn't be learned word for word. A mental map of Plavachek's travels will assist the teller in remembering the order of events. This story tells of a heroic quest, in which Plavachek undertakes a dangerous journey and restores life to several kingdoms. Child audiences usually become deeply engrossed in stories such as this, and a storyteller's use of effects such as voice characterization and gesture could be distracting.

CREATIVE DRAMATICS

Warm-up

Have the children walk in a circle, or across the room, designating the walk as the sun's daily journey. They are to make the journey as Grandfather Know-It-All does, beginning as a baby and ending as an old man, pacing themselves so that they age about eighty years during their walk. This exercise has great potential both for enhanced body awareness and for learning to draw creatively on past observations of other people. The exercise should be done slowly, and repeated as many times as the group would like.

The leader may wish to relate this walk to the riddle of the Sphinx, "What walks on four legs in the morning, two legs in the afternoon, and three legs in the evening?" (Answer: Man, who crawls as a baby, walks upright as an adult, and needs to use a cane in old age.)

Scene Play

Scenes in which the king learns that his plans have been foiled are especially enjoyable for the children to act out: the king overhearing the three Fates, the king returning home to find his daughter married to Plavachek, and the king hearing Plavachek's tale of adventure and setting off to the Black Sea. After brief planning sessions, these scenes can be acted out by groups of four or five.

CREATIVE WRITING

Movie Posters

Create the poster for a movie made from this story. Would you use the title "The Three

Golden Hairs of Grandfather Know-It-All," or would you choose a new title? Draw a picture of an exciting scene. List the major roles in the movie, and choose a star to play each role. Who will compose the music? Who will direct? You may want to include quotes from movie critics.

The leader may wish to make this a small group project in order to combine the talents of several children. A good medium for the poster is colored chalk on brown paper, with black marker for the outlines and small lettering.

Scriptwriting

Children who have experienced a series of creative dramatics activities will be ready to try their hand at scriptwriting. Their experience playing scenes has given them an ear for dialogue, and a knowledge of the importance of action. Have them choose a short scene from this story and write it in the form of a script. Scriptwriting can be accomplished most successfully by groups of three to five, with one person acting as secretary.

Before the children begin to write, they must visualize the scene as if it were a play or a movie. They list the characters in order of appearance, and describe the setting. In their script, they write the words each of the characters speak, and also describe any important actions the characters perform. This writing activity can be followed up by a performance and/or videotaping with human actors or simple puppets.

About the Tales

Each of the following annotations includes the tale's classification number or numbers as given in Margaret Read MacDonald's *The Storytellers' Sourcebook*. You may want to use this resource to locate other versions of a tale so that your students can compare them as a literature exercise. Many storytellers read all available variants of a tale they are planning to tell, and they sometimes combine elements from more than one variant in their telling. Several of the tales in this book are our own retellings, based on our research into both children's and ethnographic collections of folktale variants.

"Ticky-Picky Boom-Boom." In *Anansi, the Spider Man* by Philip M. Sherlock. New York: Crowell, 1954.

> Folktales about trickster Anansi originated in West Africa, and traveled to the New World with African slaves. "Ticky-Picky Boom-Boom" was collected on the island of Jamaica. "From Tiger to Anansi" and "Yung-Kyung-Pung," in the same collection, are also good stories to tell.
> MacDonald D983.2.1

"The Tengu's Magic Nose Fan"

> This is our retelling of a traditional Japanese folktale, combining elements from several variants.
> To learn more about tengu and badgers, see *The Very*

Special Badgers, by Claus Stamm, and *Magic Animals of Japan,* by Davis Pratt and Elsa Kula Pratt.
    MacDonald D1376.1.3.

"Buttercup"

We adapted this retelling from George Webbe Dasent's *Popular Tales from the Norse,* a translation of folktales collected by Norwegian folklorists Peter Christen Asbjørnsen and Jørgen Moe. In the Asbjørnsen and Moe tale, Buttercup tricks the troll's daughter into letting him show her how to make Buttercup broth, then cuts her head off and makes broth of her. We have tried to soften this a bit by having the daughter foolishly jump into the pot herself, a motif found in other folktales.
    MacDonald K526, G526.

"The Three Sillies"

This version is taken mainly from Joseph Jacobs' *English Folk and Fairy Tales.* We replaced a long, complicated episode in which the gentleman encounters a man who botches the housework with an anecdote about hens and boiling water from another traditional English "numskull" tale.
    Tales of foolish people abound in folklore. There are whole towns of numskulls, such as Gotham in English folklore and Chelm in Yiddish tales. Isaac Bashevis Singer's *When Schlemiel Went to Warsaw and Other Stories* is an excellent source of such stories for telling or reading aloud.
    MacDonald H1312.1.

"How Anansi Got a Small Waist"

This is our retelling, adapted for participation storytelling, of a West African folktale (variants have been collected in Liberia and Ghana). Anansi the Spider is the trickster-hero of many West African, West Indian, and Afro-American tales. Anansi is always trying to outwit his friends and neighbors; often, as in this tale, he is caught in his own trap. Among the Akan-speaking people of West Africa, the word for a certain group

of folktales told for entertainment is *anansesem*, "Anansi stories." Gail E. Haley's *A Story! A Story!* tells one version of how Anansi won ownership of all the stories.
      MacDonald A2355.1.1.2, J2183.1.3.

"Jack and the Beanstalk." In *English Folk and Fairy Tales* by Joseph Jacobs. New York: Putnam, n.d.

Folklorist Joseph Jacobs retold this story from memories of having heard it as a child in the 1860's. This is a lively and very tellable version of the familiar tale. We have made a few slight changes in wording for a modern audience. Richard Chase retells a variant of the tale from the southern United States, "Jack and the Bean Tree," in his *Jack Tales.* Raymond Briggs' humorous *Jim and the Beanstalk,* a modern picture book, follows the adventures of Jack's grandson.
      MacDonald F54.2.1.

"Baba Yaga"

This retelling is adapted from "The Witch" in Andrew Lang's *Yellow Fairy Book.*
      The delightfully macabre idiosyncrasies of Baba Yaga fascinate children. She is definitely not "just another witch." Some other Baba Yaga stories children enjoy are Ernest Small's *Baba Yaga; Anna and the Seven Swans,* retold by Maida Silverman; and "Vasilisa the Beautiful," available in many Russian folktale collections, including *Russian Folk Tales,* collected by Aleksandr Afanas'ev.

"How Fire Came to Earth"

Bob learned this tale when he was working as artist-in-the-schools in Kotzebue, Alaska; his students presented it as a shadow puppet play.
      The motif of traveling to the sky on an arrow ladder is common to many Northwest Coast Indian tribes. In several versions, some of the animals were left behind in the sky and

became the constellations. References to variants of this tale can be found in Stith Thompson's *Tales of the North American Indians*.

MacDonald A1415.

"Taily-po"

This is our retelling of a variant of a popular "catch-tale," a story that builds and builds in quiet suspense, ending as the storyteller lunges out at the audience and shouts the last few words. "The Golden Arm," and "Teeny-Tiny," both in Joseph Jacobs' *English Folk and Fairy Tales,* are well-known tales of this type. Like many tales meant to frighten, "Taily-po" is not set long ago and far away, but close to us in time and space.

MacDonald E235.4.3.2.

"The Angry Stories"

We retell this tale from several variants of the popular Korean folktale.

The moral of the tale reflects the immense importance of storytelling in traditional societies. Storytelling was (and still is, to some extent) an important part of social exchanges. Not having a story to tell was a great failing on the part of a guest; knowing stories but refusing to tell them was inexcusable. In one variant, the young man's fault was not that he stuffed stories into a bag, but that he wanted to spend his wedding night with his bride rather than tell stories to his new in-laws. For another account of the perils of not telling stories, see the Irish tale "The Man Who Had No Story," in Jane Yolen's *Favorite Folktales from Around the World.*

MacDonald M231.1.

"Briar Rose"

This tale is adapted from the collection of the Brothers Grimm. "Briar Rose," better known as "Sleeping Beauty" in the French collection of Charles Perrault (1696), is related to legends of ghostly maidens and hidden treasures in old, abandoned castles.

MacDonald D1960.3.

"The Sprightly Tailor." In *Celtic Fairy Tales* by Joseph Jacobs. New York: Putnam, 1893.

Folktales about a person who spends the night in a graveyard, or in a haunted house, are widespread. Often, this "fear test" is undertaken for the sake of a reward or in order to drive away an evil spirit once and for all. One young listener decided, after hearing this tale, that the monster "could never bother anybody again" because the tailor had succeeded in outrunning him.

MacDonald H1412.2.

"Coyote, Iktome and the Rock," told by Jenny Leading Cloud. In *American Indian Myths and Legends,* edited by Richard Erdoes and Alfonso Ortiz. New York: Pantheon, 1984.

This tale type, commonly known as "the Offended Rolling Stone," has been collected from many Native American tribes, including the Shoshone, Ute, Pawnee, Micmac, Kickapoo, Cree, Navajo, and Apache. In most variants, the stone is destroyed at the end. This particular telling is interesting in its inclusion of an episode where Coyote becomes a rug in the house of a white rancher.

MacDonald C91.9.

"The Nungwama"

Tales of a woman who escapes from a monster with the help of a series of helpful animals and/or objects are common, especially in Asia. This retelling is adapted from *Chinese Nights' Entertainment* by Adele M. Fielde. We have taken the name, "Nungwama," from another variant—the villain in Fielde's tale is a wild boar.

MacDonald K1161.3.4.

"The Pied Piper," retold by Charles Marelles. In *The Red Fairy Book* by Andrew Lang. London: Longmans, Green, 1890.

Evidently, the story of the Pied Piper has a basis in fact. Early chronicles and manuscripts tell of someone coming to the town of Hamlin, in Germany, and leaving with one hundred fifty of the town's children. And, all reports agree on the exact date: June 26, 1284. Historians have speculated that the story is based on memories of a children's crusade, an epidemic, or a mass emigration. Legends about rat-catchers existed separately, and somehow, the historical mystery of Hamlin and a legendary figure of a rat-catcher seem to have merged in the figure of the Pied Piper. The most famous English-language version of the tale is Robert Browning's poem "The Pied Piper of Hamelin."

MacDonald D1427.1.

"Wiley and the Hairy Man"

Our retelling is adapted from a folktale collected by Donnell Van de Voort for the Federal Writer's Project of the W.P.A. in Alabama.

From the references to his hooves, children quickly infer that the Hairy Man is the Devil. Most European and African variants of this tale feature a female witch as the villain. The folktale motif of the efficacy of dogs against a supernatural foe is found also in "Taily-po."

MacDonald B524.1.2.

"Suho"

Our version is a retelling inspired by several English-language versions of this Mongolian tale. "Suho" seems to be one of the "new" or "socialist" folktales that were collected and/or rewritten after the Communist revolution in China, when the government actively sought to publish tales whose heroes were common people, and which portrayed the upper classes as cruel and irrational.

MacDonald A1461.1.1.

"Why the Sea Is Salt"

Our retelling is adapted from *Popular Tales from the Norse*, by George Webbe Dasent.

According to Stith Thompson, in his book *The Folktale*, German and Scandinavian storytellers would often refer to a character as "the Devil," when they meant an ogre or troll, not the biblical Satan. In this tale, the Devil's house is above ground, not underground, and the "little devils" seem like nothing more than a typical pack of trolls. To change the name of the Devil in this tale, though, would ruin the joke of the man's taking literally his brother's instructions to "go to the Devil."

MacDonald D1651.3.1.

"The Liars' Contest." In *The Hat-Shaking Dance and Other Ashanti Tales from Ghana* by Harold Courlander and Albert Kofi Prempeh. New York: Harcourt, Brace and World, 1957.

Many tales are told of exorbitant liars and of clever liars; this is our favorite. It involves a competition of storytelling more than a liars' contest. Being a trickster as well as the legendary proprietor of all stories, Anansi quite naturally wins.

MacDonald X905.1.3. `

"The Three Golden Hairs of Grandfather Know-It-All." Our retelling is adapted from Aleksander Borejko Chodzko's *Slav Fairy Tales.*

In this variant, Grandfather Know-It-All is portrayed as the sun; he resembles other folktale cannibals with kind wives and mothers, such as the ogre in "Jack and the Beanstalk."

This story tells of a quest: a young person of lowly birth becomes a hero by travelling into dangerous, unknown territory and bringing back or restoring a treasure. Older children are particularly fond of this type of folktale. A good quest tale with a heroine is the Norwegian folktale "East of the Sun, West of the Moon," available in many collections.

MacDonald H1273.2.

More Stories and Poems
for Telling, Creative Dramatics,
and Creative Writing

Many of the following stories and poems are also available in other collections and single editions.

"The Adventures of Isabel" in *Custard and Company* by Ogden Nash. Boston: Little, Brown, 1980.

This poem about a brave and resourceful girl who defeats a bear, a witch, a giant, and a doctor makes a good pair mime to accompanying narration. Young poets can attempt a fifth adventure in which Isabel meets another dangerous character.

Alligators All Around by Maurice Sendak. New York: Harper and Row, 1962.

The alphabetical antics of this rambunctious alligator family make a gigglesome mime activity. Use this book as inspiration for writing and illustrating other action alphabets.

"Alligator's Sunday Suit" in *Bo Rabbit Smart for True: Folktales from the Gullah* by Priscilla Jaquith. New York: Philomel, 1981.

Brer Rabbit shows Brer Alligator and his too-perfect family just what trouble is. In creative dramatics some of the children can play the alligator and his wife, sons, and daughters, while others play the ring-of fire.

Anansi the Spider, adapted by Gerald McDermott. New York: Holt, Rinehart, 1972.

Each of Anansi's six children possesses a special skill, and each skill comes in handy when father Anansi falls into the river and is swallowed by a fish. This African folktale is easy to act out in its entirety. The claims by each son—that *he* played the most important part in the rescue—can be the basis of a creative writing activity in which children write from the point of view of one of Anansi's sons.

"Anansi's Hat-Shaking Dance" in *The Hat-Shaking Dance and Other Ashanti Tales from Ghana* by Harold Courlander and Albert Kofi Prempeh. New York: Harcourt, Brace and World, 1957.

Anansi tries to prove that he can fast longer than anyone else. Children will enjoy improvising his frantic "hat-shaking dance." Courlander and Prempeh's version is excellent for storytelling, and it can be enlivened by the chants in "Today is Shake-Head Day" from *Singing Tales of Africa,* retold by Adjai Robinson (New York: Scribner's, 1974).

Anna and the Seven Swans, retold by Maida Silverman. New York: Morrow, 1984.

Anna's baby brother is carried off by the seven swan servants of Baba Yaga. Less frightening than the Baba Yaga tale included in this book, *Anna and the Seven Swans* is nonetheless exciting to hear and fun to act out, and it includes color illustrations of Baba Yaga and her house on chicken legs.

"Ayele and the Flowers" in *Singing Tales of Africa,* retold by Adjai Robinson. New York: Scribner's, 1974.

> Ayele and her friends become lost while picking flowers. They sing a song to help their mothers find them (words and musical notation are included). This short story provides good creative dramatics material for an all-girl group. The song can easily be played on a recorder or a small xylophone.

"Barney McCabe" in *Just Enough to Make a Story* by Nancy Schimmel. Berkeley, Calif.: Sisters' Choice Press, 1982. Also recorded by David Holt on *The Hairyman and Other Wild Tales.* Weston, Conn.: Weston Woods, 1981.

> "Barney McCabe" is a *cante-fable,* a story that is partly told and partly sung (storytellers need more of these). The language in David Holt's version is the more contemporary. Children can easily learn the tale's three short songs and sing them with the storyteller.

The Bremen Town Musicians, retold by Paul Galdone from the collection of the Brothers Grimm. New York: McGraw-Hill, 1968.

> Rejected by their owners, an old donkey, dog, cat, and rooster set off for the town of Bremen to be town musicians. The storyteller can divide the audience into four groups— donkeys, dogs, cats, and roosters—to form an animal orchestra and lead a concert by the Bremen town musicians.

"Brer Rabbit and the Tar Baby" in *Tales of Uncle Remus,* retold by Julius Lester. New York: Dial, 1987.

> Brer Rabbit's famous encounter with the tar baby makes a wonderful mime—and not an easy one! Children may attempt it during the storytelling. As a creative dramatics activity, pairs of children can improvise the scene in which

Brer Rabbit tries to convince Brer Wolf to throw him into the briar patch.

"Brer Rabbit and the Mosquitoes" in *Tales of Uncle Remus,* retold by Julius Lester. New York: Dial, 1987.

Brer Rabbit fools Brer Wolf in a short and highly enjoyable audience-participation story.

"Coyote and the Lizards" in *Coyote Stories of the Navajo People* by Robert A. Roessel, Jr., and Dillon Platero. Rough Rock, Arizona: Rough Rock Demonstration School, 1974.

Foolish Coyote insists on playing the lizards' dangerous rock-sliding games. Skateboarders will enjoy miming Coyote's catastrophic downhill ride.

A Crocodile's Tale, adapted by Jose Aruego. New York: Scholastic, 1975.

A crocodile captures Juan but promises to let him go, uneaten, if the boy can find one creature who believes in gratitude. This short tale can be acted out in its entirety by a group or groups of four to six children.

D'Aulaire's Trolls by Ingri and Edgar Parin D'Aulaire. New York: Doubleday, 1972.

Children can learn all about trolls while acting out these short anecdotes about the imaginary creatures.

Desert Voices by Byrd Baylor. New York: Macmillan, 1981.

Byrd Baylor's poetic yet realistic descriptions of the lives of desert creatures can be used to inspire mime and the writing of similar pieces about other animals.

The Emperor's New Clothes by Hans Christian Andersen, retold by Anne Rockwell. New York: Crowell, 1982.

> The work of the weavers is, after all, nothing but mime—and there are many other scenes in this tale that are just right for creative dramatics, for example, the reactions of the king's courtiers to the invisible cloth and the final parade through town.

The Exploding Frog and Other Fables from Aesop, retold by John McFarland. Boston: Little, Brown, 1981.

> Aesop's fables are easy and enjoyable to act out. Exact language is important, so dramatics should ideally be performed to a reading of the fable.

Five Chinese Brothers, retold by Claire Hutchet Bishop. New York: Coward, McCann, 1938.

> The illustrations in this book have been criticized for their negative stereotypes; however, the words of the story can still be shared for their excellent creative writing and creative dramatics potential. Children choose and play sea creatures in an introductory mime activity. Then, when the first son swallows the sea, they are all beached on dry land until he releases it.

Fortunately by Remy Charlip. New York: Parents, 1964.

> This hilarious series of misadventures is highly enjoyable to act out in solo mime and provides an excellent model for inventing another series of similar misadventures.

Frederick by Leo Lionni. New York: Pantheon, 1967.

> Frederick the mouse is a poet; while the other mice gather food for the winter, Frederick gathers images. Children enjoy

acting out the changing attitude of the other mice toward Frederick—first rejection and ridicule, then admiration and gratitude. As a creative writing project, have the children write a poem that Frederick might recite to cheer up the cold, hungry mice during the winter.

The Funny Little Woman by Arlene Mosel. New York: Dutton, 1972.

Children enjoy playing the parts of the wise statues and of the monstrous Oni in this Japanese folktale. As a creative dramatics or creative writing project, have the children tell what might happen if an evil or foolish person made this underground journey.

The Golden Goose, retold by William Stobbs from the collection of the Brothers Grimm. New York: McGraw-Hill, 1967.

Simpleton's kindness brings him a golden goose, whose magical property is to make all who touch it stick fast. The scene of Simpleton walking along, followed by a long procession of people stuck tight to each other, is quite laughable—in fact, it wins for him as wife the celebrated "Princess-who-never-laughed."

The Great Minu, retold by Beth P. Wilson. Chicago: Follett, 1974. Also available as "Younde Goes to Town" in *The Cow-Tail Switch and Other Tales from Nigeria* by Harold Courlander and George Herzog. New York: Holt, 1947.

A poor farmer in Ghana travels to the great modern city of Accra for the first time. Though he does not speak or understand the language of Accra, the farmer learns an important lesson when all the people he meets respond to his questions by answering *minu,* "I don't understand."

The Gunniwolf, retold by Wilhelmina Harper. New York: Dutton, 1967. Also available in *The Flannel Board Storytelling Book* by Judy Sierra. New York: H. W. Wilson, 1987.

In this Afro-American folktale, a girl escapes the great grey gunniwolf by putting him to sleep with a song. This tale can be used as a narrated pair mime and as a model for writing a similar story about another little child and a different frightening monster.

Hee Haw by Anne McGovern. Boston: Houghton, Mifflin, 1969.

This adaptation of the La Fontaine fable "The Miller, the Boy and the Donkey" cautions against blindly following others' advice. Have a large pillow or duffel bag play the role of the donkey.

Horton Hatches the Egg by Dr. Seuss. New York: Random, 1940.

This story in verse can be played in scenes, or all the way through, as the leader reads or recites the text. It offers excellent opportunities for mime and a flexible number of roles to accommodate a large group.

"Hungry Spider and the Turtle" in *The Cow-Tail Switch and Other Tales from Nigeria* by Harold Courlander and George Herzog. New York: Holt, 1947.

Anansi is clever, but low and slow Turtle is his equal in this exchange of poor hospitality. The story makes a good pair mime: pairs of children act the parts of Turtle and Anansi as the leader reads or tells the story. Character mimes can also be incorporated into participation storytelling.

It Could Always Be Worse: A Yiddish Folktale, adapted by Margot Zemach. New York: Farrar, Straus, 1977.

When the small noises in his house bother a man, the rabbi advises him to take in first one, then another, of his farm animals. Before telling the story, divide the audience into five parts (chickens, roosters, geese, goats, cows), and give each section an animal noise to make whenever they hear the name of that animal in the story. This sort of participation storytelling is enjoyably silly, and great fun for family audiences.

The Judge by Margot Zemach. New York: Farrar, Strauss, 1969.

Despite its picture book format, *The Judge* is a fable for older children. Read or tell the story several times, until the children know the cumulative poem about this monster:

A horrible thing is coming our way,
Creeping closer day by day . . .

The story can be acted out in its entirety, with a group of children playing the monster that eats the judge. The court-room scene can be expanded with children playing the parts of lawyers, bailiffs, jury, etc.

"Lazy Tok," retold by Mervyn Skipper in *A Storyteller's Choice,* edited by Eileen Colwell. New York: Walck, 1964.

Long a favorite of storytellers, "Lazy Tok," a folktale from Borneo, is fun to act out in small groups, with children playing the parts of the tree, the basket, and Tok's other servants—or as a mime in which all the children simultaneously play the role of Tok as the storyteller narrates.

"The Leopard's Daughter," retold by Harold Courlander in *With a Deep Sea Smile,* edited by Virginia Tashjian. Boston: Little, Brown, 1974.

> Any number of children can play the roles of the animals who try to win the hand of the leopard's daughter in marriage in this folktale from Liberia. The group also has the opportunity to create their own, original "dance of war" and "dance of peace" for the story.

A Light in the Attic by Shel Silverstein. New York: Harper and Row, 1981.

> "Ladies First," "Squishy Touch," and "Homework Machine" are especially good for creative dramatics.

The Magic Wings: A Tale from China, retold by Diane Wolkstein. New York: Dutton, 1983.

> A delightful story of women and girls who want more than anything to fly. As a creative writing project, have the children write a sequel to the story, telling about the further adventures of the little goose girl.

"Masters of All Masters" in *English Folk and Fairy Tales* by Joseph Jacobs. New York: G. P. Putnam's Sons, n.d.

> A tale and a tongue twister in one, "Master of All Masters" can be acted out in pairs simultaneously. Other tongue twisters, or making up silly names for everyday things, are good follow-up activities.

Millions of Cats by Wanda Gag. New York: Coward, McCann, 1928.

> There are plenty of cat roles and opportunities for cat pantomimes and choral participation in Wanda Gag's story of an old man in search of a pet.

Obedient Jack, adapted by Paul Galdone from the collection of the Brothers Grimm. New York: Watts, 1972.

> Jack faithfully follows his mother's instructions to the letter in this English folktale. Unfortunately, he always follows the instructions for the *previous task,* with hilarious results. Children can simultaneously mime Jack's role, as the leader plays Jack's mother (or father).

"The Sloogeh Dog and the Stolen Aroma" in *Tales from the Story Hat: African Folktales* by Verna Aardema. New York: Coward, McCann, 1960.

> A greedy rich man accuses the sloogeh dog of stealing the smell of his food. The trial of the dog provides an opportunity for children to enact and elaborate upon the courtroom scene.

"The Stepchild and the Fruit Trees" in *Singing Tales of Africa,* retold by Adjai Robinson. New York: Scribner's, 1974.

> The songs in this book make the tales ideal for participation storytelling. In this story, a mistreated stepdaughter gains her independence not through marriage, but through her own magic songs.

Stone Soup, adapted by Marcia Brown. New York: Scribner's, 1947.

> Trickery which benefits everyone is the theme of this French variant of a well-known folktale. The townsfolk can fill a huge, imaginary cooking pot and brew up a tubful of stone soup for everyone. The fact that the soldiers and the townsfolk are each trying to fool each other provides highly effective stimulus for creative dramatics.

The Stonecutter, adapted by Gerald McDermott. New York: Viking, 1975.

This familiar Japanese folktale can be acted out with each child playing the part of the stonecutter, going through his series of transformations. The storyteller narrates, and can use wood blocks for the sound of the stonecutting tools. McDermott leaves the story tantalizingly unfinished; children can create their own ending in drama or in writing.

The Story of Ferdinand by Munro Leaf. New York: Viking, 1938.

The bullfight scene, in which Ferdinand foils the matador by refusing to fight, can be played by a large group of children in pantomime to the reading of the text. A circle of chairs can form the bullfight arena.

The Story of Paul Bunyan, retold by Barbara Emberley. Englewood Cliffs, N.J.: Prentice-Hall, 1963.

Children enjoy pantomiming the activities of giants, and this particular version of the Paul Bunyan story provides a good text for miming the amazing feats of Paul and his men. Is Paul Bunyan responsible for some giant landmark, natural or man-made, in your part of the country?

"The Story of the Three Little Pigs" in *English Folk and Fairy Tales* by Joseph Jacobs. New York: G. P. Putnam, n.d.

This tale is always fun to dramatize, and older children may choose to parody it. In this version, the third pig tricks the wolf not once but three times.

"The Strange Visitor" in *English Folk and Fairy Tales* by Joseph Jacobs. New York: G. P. Putnam, n.d.

A visitor comes down the chimney of the old woman's house, piece by piece. Children can make the body of the strange visitor on the floor, shaping their bodies into the form of his feet, legs, knees, etc., and speak his eerie lines in unison.

"The Tale of Custard the Dragon" in *Custard and Company* by Ogden Nash. Boston: Little, Brown, 1980.

Belinda's pet dragon, Custard, is even more cowardly than her little mouse, Blink, until a bloodthirsty pirate breaks into their house. Nash's rhythmic and clever poetry inspires wonderful mimes.

Three Strong Women: A Tall Tale from Japan by Claus Stamm. New York: Viking, 1962.

A great Sumo wrestler must take lessons from a young girl, her mother, and her grandmother, who are all much stronger than he! In the dramatics each child mimes the great wrestling feats of the three strong women.

The Three Wishes, retold by Paul Galdone from the collection of the Brothers Grimm. New York: McGraw-Hill, 1969.

A man and woman waste their three wishes. This tale is a good resource for creative writing. Are there three wishes that would make *you* happy?

Toad is the Uncle of Heaven: A Vietnamese Folktale, retold by Jeanne M. Lee. New York: Holt, 1985.

Because of a drought, the toad travels to ask the king of heaven for rain. He takes with him some bees, a rooster, and a tiger, who create such havoc that the king grants their request. Now, the toad has only to croak to let the king know that the earth needs rain. Besides scene play, the story can be used as a stimulus for miming activities in the rain.

"Urashima Taro and the Princess of the Sea," in *The Dancing Kettle and Other Japanese Folk Tales,* retold by Yoshiko Uchida. New York: Harcourt, Brace, 1949.

Urashima is kind to an old sea turtle, who in turn carries him down to the kingdom at the bottom of the sea. A compelling image of this story is that of the magic doors that reveal to Urashima the passage of the seasons on earth. These suggest creative dramatic activities in which children mime activities or feelings associated with each season.

The Wave, retold by Margaret Hodges. New York: Houghton Mifflin, 1964.

Ojiisan saves the people of a Japanese village from the great tidal wave that follows an earthquake. Children can play both the natural drama (acting as buildings and the wave) and then the human drama. What happened after the end of the story? Possibilities can be explored in writing or dramatics.

Who's in Rabbit's House? A Masai Tale, retold by Verna Aardema. New York: Dial, 1977.

Though the book reads like a script, and the illustrations show masked actors playing the story, this tale works best when you let the children improvise their lines and play the roles as if they were animals.

Bibliography of Works Consulted

Aardema, Verna. *Ji-Nongo-Nongo Means Riddles*. New York: Four Winds, 1978.

Aarne, Antti, and Stith Thompson. *The Types of the Folktale*. Folklore Fellows Communications, 184. Helsinki: Academia Scientiarum Fennica, 1973.

Afanas'ev, Alekandr, comp. *Russian Fairy Tales*. New York: Pantheon, 1945.

Barker, W. H., and C. Sinclair. *West African Folk-Tales*. London: G. G. Harrap & Co., 1917.

Botkin, B. A. *Treasury of American Folklore*. New York: Crown, 1944.

Briggs, Katherine, ed. *A Dictionary of British Folk-Tales in the English Language*. 2 vols. Bloomington: Indiana University Press, 1970.

Briggs, Raymond. *Jim and the Beanstalk*. New York: Coward-McCann, 1970.

Bruchac, Joseph. *Iroquois Stories*. Trumansburg, N.Y.: Crossing Press, 1985.

Chase, Richard. *Jack Tales*. New York: Houghton Mifflin, 1943.

Chodzko, Aleksander Borejko. *Slav Fairy Tales*. New York: A. L. Burt, 1905.

Choy, In Hak. *A Type Index of Korean Folk Tales.* Seoul: Myong Ji University, 1979.

Courlander, Harold, and Albert Kofi Prempeh. *The Hat-Shaking Dance and Other Ashanti Tales from Ghana.* New York: Harcourt, Brace and World, 1957.

Dasent, George Webbe. *Popular Tales from the Norse.* New York: Putnam, 1908.

D'Aulaire, Ingri, and Edgar Parin. *D'Aulaire's Trolls.* New York: Doubleday, 1972.

Delarue, Paul, and Marie-Louise Tenèze. *Le Conte populaire français.* 3 vols. Paris: Éditions Érasme, 1957.

DeWit, Dorothy. *The Talking Stone: An Anthology of Native American Tales and Legends.* New York: Greenwillow, 1979.

Eberhard, Wolfram. *Folktales of China.* Chicago: University of Chicago Press, 1965.

Erdoes, Richard, and Alfonso Ortiz, ed. *American Indian Myths and Legends.* New York: Pantheon, 1984.

Fielde, Adele M. *Chinese Nights' Entertainment.* New York: Putnam, 1893.

Greene, Ellin, and George Shannon. *Storytelling: A Selected, Annotated Bibliography.* New York: Garland, 1986.

Grimm, Jacob and Wilhelm. *Complete Grimm's Fairy Tales.* New York: Pantheon, 1944.

Haley, Gail E. *A Story! A Story!* New York: Atheneum. 1970.

Ikeda, Hirolo. *A Type and Motif Index of Japanese Folk-Literature.* Folklore Fellows Communications 209. Helsinki: Academia Scientiarum Fennica, 1971.